**Crayola**

# Dream~Makers®
Building fun and creativity into standards-based learning

# Language Arts
K through 6

Ron De Long, M.Ed.
Janet B. McCracken, M.Ed.
Elizabeth Willett, M.Ed.

D1265257

Crayola

A Hallmark Company

© 2009 Crayola, LLC
Easton, PA 18044-0431

# Acknowledgements

This guide and the entire Crayola® Dream-Makers® series would not be possible without the expertise and tireless efforts of Ron De Long, Jan McCracken, and Elizabeth Willett. Your passion for children, the arts, and creativity are inspiring. Thank you. Special thanks also to Bonnie Saunders for her content-area expertise, writing, research, and curriculum development of this guide.

**Crayola also gratefully acknowledges the teachers and students who tested the lessons in this guide:**

Barbie Bailey-Smith, Little River Elementary School, Durham, NC

Susan Bivona, Mount Prospect Elementary School, Basking Ridge, NJ

Jennifer Braun, Oak Street Elementary School, Basking Ridge, NJ

Lori Crossley, Round Hills Elementary School, Williamsport, PA

Regina DeFrancisco, Liberty Corner Elementary School and Mount Prospect Elementary School, Basking Ridge, NJ

Sadie Everett, Jordan Community School, Chicago, IL

Keith Giard, Northeast Elementary School, Vernon, CT

Felicitas Harrig, Oakhurst Elementary School, Fort Worth, TX

Kathleen Hull, Rockway Elementary School, Rockway, FL

Craig Hinshaw, Hillar Elementary School, Madison Heights, MI

Christy Holloran, Alexander Elementary School, Houston, TX

Shari Kaucher, South Mountain Middle School, Allentown, PA

Linda Kondikoff, Asa Packer Elementary School, Bethlehem, PA

Kamyee Ladas, Mount Prospect Elementary School, Basking Ridge, NJ

Romona Lapsley, Mountainside Elementary School, Fort Carson, CO

Sandy Lerman, Poinciana Math-Science-Technology Magnet Elementary School, Boynton Beach, FL

Elyse Martin, Jordan Community School, Chicago, IL

Rebecca J. Martin, Oakhurst Elementary School, Fort Worth, TX

Rebecca Murphy, Mount Prospect Elementary School, Basking Ridge, NJ

Marcy Muellar, Alexander Elementary School, Houston, TX

Diane Myers, Oakhurst Elementary School, Fort Worth, TX

Nancy Knutsen, Triangle School, Hillsborough, NJ

Jessica Patterson, Tanglewood Elementary School, Fort Worth, TX

Marcia Elise Peterson-Effinger, Alton Elementary School, Brenham, TX

Julie Piazza, St. Jane Frances De Chantal School, Easton, PA

Nancy Rhoads, Curlew Creek Elementary School, Clearwater, FL

Rosie Riordan, Sunflower Elementary School, Lenexa, KS

Therese Sadlier, Hillar Elementary School, Madison Heights, MI

Patricia Skalka, Holly Glen Elementary School, Williamstown, NJ

Neila P. Steiner, Community School District 102, Bronx, NY

Eleni Strawn, Curlew Creek Elementary School, Clearwater, FL

Sandra Young, Jackson Elementary School, Williamsport, PA

Bobbi Yancey, College Oaks Elementary School, Lake Charles, LA

Barbara Yanoshek, Klatt Elementary School, Anchorage, AK

Paula Zelienka, St. John Neumann Regional School, Palmerton, PA

The education community knows that language arts and vocabulary skills are only strengthened by expanding children's literacy skills beyond reading, writing, and speaking to include listening skills and visual literacy. As a supplemental curriculum resource, we developed and tested these lessons to stimulate your students' imaginations and creativity in exploring "beyond the book" to discover more about themselves, their world, our past, and future. Only with a strong sense of curiosity and wonder that both language and visual arts inspire can our children make their own dreams become real.

Nancy A. De Bellis
Director, Education Marketing
Crayola

Crayola Dream-Makers is a series of standards-based supplemental curriculum resources that contain lesson plans for educators teaching kindergarten through 6th grade. Each guide uses visual art lessons to stimulate critical thinking and problem-solving for individual subject areas such as Math, Language Arts, Science, and Social Studies. Students demonstrate and strengthen their knowledge while engaging in creative, fun, hands-on learning processes.

# Table of Contents

Each Crayola Dream-Makers guide provides elementary classroom and art teachers with 24 arts-focused lessons that extend children's learning and enhance academic skills. Align these lessons with your school district and state curriculum standards. Stay flexible in your teaching approaches with adaptations like these.

- **Be prepared.** Read through the lesson first. Create an art sample so you understand the process.
- **Discover new resources.** Each lesson contains background information, fine art and craft examples, representative student artwork, vocabulary builders, and discussion ideas. Use these suggestions as a springboard to find resources that address your students' interests and are pertinent to your community. Search Web sites such as Google Image to locate fine art. Stretch student imaginations and their awareness of the world around them.
- **Seek creative craft materials.** Ask children's families and local businesses to recycle clean, safe items for project use and take better care of the environment, too. **Recycle, Reuse, Renew!**
- **Showcase student achievements.** Create banners to accompany curriculum project displays in your class, school, or community. Post the lesson's standards-based objectives with displays to demonstrate broad-based student learning. Demonstrate how children's accomplishments have personal meaning and promote life-long learning through portfolio documentation.
- **Make this book your own.** Jot down your own ideas as you plan and reflect on students' learning experiences. Combine art techniques and lesson content to fit goals for your students and classroom. Substitute other transformative craft materials. With students, make content webs of possibilities for extending learning opportunities.
- **Build connections.** Collaborate with your students, other teachers, administrators, artists in residence, and community groups to plan lessons that are unique. Work together to promote creative thinking!
- **Write DREAM statements.** As part of the assessment process, students are asked to reflect on their work in a dream journal. Before the lesson, Dream statements are expected to capture children's prior knowledge about each topic. After each lesson, students state in writing how they will use what they have learned and dream about possibilities for future exploration.
- **Funding resources.** Crayola Dream-Makers lesson plans have been used in school programs funded by a variety of federal, state, local, and private grants. For more information about grants and grant writing visit The Foundation Center at www.fdncenter.org.

The lessons in this book are intended to address content benchmarks and grade-level expectations in language arts along with a heavy concentration of key art concepts. All lessons are teacher- and student-tested and follow a consistent format to support you in planning creative, fun learning opportunities for your students.

## Benefits of Arts Integration

The 2006 report *Critical Evidence—How the ARTS Benefit Student Achievement*, published by the National Assembly of State Arts Agencies in collaboration with the Arts Education Partnership, identifies a number of ways that arts learning experiences benefit students. Teachers who consciously integrate arts-based practice into their teaching bring these benefits to their students.

> "Certain arts activities promote growth in positive social skills, including self-confidence, self-control, conflict resolution, collaboration, empathy, and social tolerance. Research evidence demonstrates these benefits apply to all students, not just the gifted and talented. The arts can play a key role in developing social competencies among educationally or economically disadvantaged youth who are at greatest risk of not successfully completing their education." (p. 14)

According to Diane Watanabe and Richard Sjolseth, co-directors of the Institute of Learning, Teaching, and the Human Brain, when there is joy in learning, student achievement soars.

> "When students find joy in their creative outlets, there is a positive carryover to school in general. Emotion, interest, and motivation promote learning and memory. Brain research shows the brain produces at least three pleasure chemicals when joy is present: endorphins, dopamine, and serotonin. These chemicals account for the emotional states produced by self-satisfaction, positive self-image, passion for one's art, and joy in learning." (2006, p. 20)

## Children learn in many different ways

Howard Gardner has identified eight types of intelligences and may add others. Arts-integrated learning experiences enable children to more fully develop a wide range of skills and understandings.

- **Linguistic intelligence** involves sensitivity to spoken and written language, the ability to learn languages, and the capacity to use language to accomplish certain goals.
- **Logical-mathematical intelligence** consists of the capacity to analyze problems logically, carry out mathematical operations, and investigate issues scientifically.
- **Musical intelligence** involves skill in the performance, composition, and appreciation of musical patterns.
- **Bodily-kinesthetic intelligence** entails the potential of using one's whole body or parts of the body to solve problems.
- **Spatial intelligence** involves the potential to recognize and use the patterns of wide space and more confined areas.
- **Interpersonal intelligence** is concerned with the capacity to understand the intentions, motivations, and desires of other people. It allows people to work effectively with others.
- **Intrapersonal intelligence** entails the capacity to understand oneself, to appreciate one's feelings, fears, and motivations.
- **Naturalist intelligence** enables human beings to recognize, categorize, and draw upon certain features of the environment. (Gardner, 1999: pp. 41-43, 52)

## Find More Resources at www.crayola.com/educators

Supplementary materials for Dream-Makers guides include:

- Printable certificates for recognizing children's participation and adults' support
- Thousands of images of children's art
- Demonstration videos for teaching arts-integrated lessons
- Printable resource guides for educators and administrators
- More than 1,000 free, cross-curricular lesson plan ideas on wide-ranging topics, all developed by experienced educators. Sign up for free monthly newsletters to keep you abreast of the newest Crayola products, events, and projects.

## Bibliography

Gardner, H. (1999). *Intelligence Reframed: Multiple Intelligences for the 21st Century.* New York: Basic Books.

Marzano, R.J. (March 2005). *ASCD Report–Preliminary Report on the 2004-05 Evaluation Study of the ASCD Program for Building Academic Vocabulary.* Reston, VA: Association for Supervision and Curriculum Development.

National Assembly of State Arts Agencies (NASAA) in collaboration with the Arts Education Partnership. (2006). *Critical Evidence–How the ARTS Benefit Student Achievement.* Washington, DC: Author.

Smith, M.K. (2002). Howard Gardner and multiple intelligences. The encyclopedia of informal education, http://www.infed.org/thinkers/gardner.htm. Retrieved from http://www.infed.org/thinkers/gardner.htm May 9, 2007. Reprinted with permission.

Watanabe, D., & Sjolseth, R. (2006). *Lifetime Payoffs: The Positive Effect of the Arts on Human Brain Development.* Miami, FL: NFAA youngARTS. Reprinted with permission.

# Birds of a Feather

## Objectives

Students read a wide range of fiction and nonfiction texts to conduct research on birds and related environmental issues.

Students (K-4) employ a variety of modeling techniques to create, decorate, and display 3-dimensional birds inspired by their reading.

Students (5-6) look at and create a bird drawing reflective of the style of Audubon.

## Multiple Intelligences

Bodily-kinesthetic
Interpersonal
Linguistic
Naturalist

## What Does It Mean?

**Knead:** work clay into a uniform mixture by pressing, folding, and stretching

**Marbleize:** knead at least two colors a little to achieve a marble effect

## National Standards

**Visual Arts Standard #1**
Understanding and applying media, techniques, and processes

**Visual Arts Standard #6**
Making connections between visual arts and other disciplines

**English Language Arts Standard #1**
Students read a wide range of print and non-print texts to build an understanding of texts, of themselves, and of the cultures of the United States and the world; to acquire new information; to respond to the needs and demands of society and the workplace; and for personal fulfillment. Among these texts are fiction and nonfiction, classic and contemporary works.

**English Language Arts Standard #3**
Students apply a wide range of strategies to comprehend, interpret, evaluate, and appreciate texts. They draw on their prior experience, their interactions with other readers and writers, their knowledge of word meaning and of other texts, their word identification strategies, and their understanding of textual features (e.g., sound-letter correspondence, sentence structure, context graphics).

**English Language Arts Standard #7**
Students conduct research on issues and interests by generating ideas and questions, and by posing problems. They gather, evaluate, and synthesize data from a variety of sources (e.g., print and non-print texts, artifacts, people) to communicate their discoveries in ways that suit their purpose and audience.

## Background Information

Birds come in many colors, shapes, and sizes. They have many different behaviors and ways to communicate, too. The mourning dove makes a cooing, calming sound. The blue jay has blue, black, and white feathers and can be a bully. The Northern cardinal lives along woodland edges, thickets, gardens, and parks. Males are much brighter red than females. Northern orioles eat insects, fruits, and seeds. Red-winged blackbirds make their homes in marshes, hayfields, pastures, orchards, and yards. Redheaded woodpeckers are often heard tapping into trees, searching for food.

Many birds have become endangered due to environmental issues. In 1973, the U.S. Congress enacted the Endangered Species Act to help save some of the most imperiled birds and wildlife. The National Audubon Society is working to assure that Congress and the public continue to support this act as well as other wildlife and conservation programs that affect birds. One way to participate is to take part in the Audubon Society's Annual Christmas Bird Count or the Great Backyard Bird Count.

## Resources

*Audubon: Painter of Birds in the Wild Frontier* by Jennifer Armstrong
Biography of the famous naturalist well suited to grades 2 to 4. Illustrations provide information and inspiration.

*Feathers for Lunch* by Lois Ehlert
Lively picture book about a cat in search of lunch. Appeals to primary students. Detailed drawings and information about 12 common backyard birds.

*Hoot* by Carl Hiaasen

Three teenagers on a mission to save a nest of baby owls from a developer's bulldozer. Good springboard for discussions about environmental issues in middle school classrooms.

*http://www.audubon.org*
An excellent resource for all ages. Text and photos regarding numerous species as well as information about conservation efforts and special programs.

## Vocabulary List

*Use this list to explore new vocabulary, create idea webs, or brainstorm related subjects. Focus on the words most appropriate for the children in your group.*

| | | |
|---|---|---|
| Banding | Fledging | Preen |
| Beak | Flock | Raptor |
| Binoculars | Form | Roost |
| Blend | Habitat | Species |
| Color mixing | Join | Tail |
| Conservation | Marbleize | Wetlands |
| Crest | Migration | Wing |
| Crop | Molt | Wingspan |
| Endangered | Ornithology | |
| Environment | Plumage | |
| Feathers | | |

Artwork by students from Mt. Prospect Elementary School, Basking Ridge, New Jersey.
Teachers: Susan Bivona, Regina DeFrancisco, Kamyee Ladas

Artwork by students from
Oakhurst Elementary School, Fort Worth, Texas.
Teacher: Diane Myers
and
students from Jackson Elementary School,
Williamsport, Pennsylvania.
Teacher: Sandra Young

Artwork by students from St.
Theresa School,
Hellertown, Pennsylvania.

Crayola Dream~Makers®
Building fun and creativity into standards-based learning

# Birds of a Feather

| | K-2 | 3-4 | 5-6 |
|---|---|---|---|
| **Suggested Preparation and Discussion** | Display a variety of books and pictures of birds as well as sample bird sculptures.<br><br>Invite a local bird expert to make a presentation designed to capture children's imaginations about local birds. | Read a book about birds appropriate to the ages, interests, and ability levels of the students. Examine bird illustrations and discuss details that make various species of birds different from one another.<br><br>Observe birds in local bird sanctuaries, at bird feeders, and elsewhere within the environment. Learn more about their habitats, food, and habits. | Write the word *ornithology* for all to see. Who knows what it means? Discuss the definition and various aspects of the study of birds. How many species are there? Which are endangered? Why? What organizations are trying to save them? How? What can individuals do to help with bird conservation efforts?<br><br>Read *Hoot* aloud with the class. It will take several weeks, so encourage students to refer to the Audubon Society Web site and other references during this time to broaden their knowledge of birds and conservation issues.<br><br>Discuss Audubon's bird illustrations to discover how Audubon created detailed illustrations of birds in their habitats. |
| **Crayola® Supplies** | • Glitter Glue<br>• Washable Markers | • Paint Brushes    • Tempera Paint<br>• Watercolors | • Colored Pencils<br>• Erasable Colored Pencils |
| | • Model Magic®    • School Glue    • Scissors | | |
| **Other Materials** | • Paper clips (large)<br>• Ribbon, string, or yarn | • Corrugated cardboard<br>• Raffia, feathers, or other natural materials | • White drawing paper |
| | • Coffee stirrers<br>• Modeling tools such as craft sticks, plastic dinnerware, and wood toothpicks<br>• Recycled milk carton or similar container    • Stones or sand<br>• Tree branch | | |
| **Set-up/Tips** | • Find a tree branch without leaves. Secure branch in a sturdy container with stones or sand.<br>• Model Magic compound fresh from the pack sticks to itself. | | |
| **Process: Session 1 30-45 min.** | 1. Select a bird to model. Look at pictures of the bird and study details of the species. | | |
| | 2. Knead modeling compound into a sphere a little bigger than a ping-pong ball. Experiment with mixing different colors. Blend two primary colors to create a secondary color. Blend colors with white to make tints. Experiment with kneading color from washable markers into white compound to create unique colors. Produce a marbled effect by blending several colors.<br>3. Make basic geometric forms such as cubes, cones, and spheres for the bird's body.<br>4. Flatten some compound. Cut additional forms to add to the body such as wings, beaks, tails, and feathers. Press and smooth forms firmly onto the body.<br>5. Insert toothpicks or coffee stirrers into adjacent pieces for added support as needed. Use dots of glue if the pieces are dry to the touch.<br>6. Etch details and texture using modeling tools.<br>7. Press a large paper clip into the top of each bird for hanging (K-2 only). Air-dry birds 24 hours. | | 2. Draw the bird in its environment. Erase to adjust.<br>3. Fill in the contour line shapes of the bird and its environment with a first layer of color.<br>4. Apply additional layers of pencil color over the first layer to blend colors that reflect authentic details of the bird. White colored pencil applied over darker colors helps to create soft pastel effects.<br>5. Add detail to the bird drawing so it reflects the character of an Audubon drawing. |

| | K-2 | 3-4 | 5-6 |
|---|---|---|---|
| **Process: Session 2 10-15 min.** | 8. Cut yarn. Tie on paper clips. Hang birds on twigs to create a class flock. Decorate birds with Glitter Glue if desired. Air-dry glue. | 8. Watercolor the birds to define features and colors. Air-dry the paint. | 6. Share observations about the drawing experience. What blending and drawing techniques worked well? What problems occurred and how were they resolved? What facts can the student share with the class about the species drawn? Use new vocabulary. |
| **Process: Session 3 30-45 min.** | 9. Share observations about the experience of making the birds. What techniques worked well? What problems occurred and how were they resolved? 10. Students show their birds and describe how they created their models. Share facts and use new vocabulary. | 9. Glue bird models to corrugated cardboard. Glue grasses, stones, twigs, or other found natural materials to create a habitat around the bird. Air-dry glue. 10. Write descriptive paragraphs about bird models. Challenge students to include descriptive adjectives. 11. Display models. Students read their descriptive paragraphs to the group. | 7. Ask students to imagine they were their birds. Write a paragraph that describes what they would see from a bird's-eye view. |
| **Assessment** | • Compare the child's bird model to the reference picture. Was attention paid to details? Does the finished product demonstrate the student understands modeling techniques? <br> • Did the child accurately describe unique features of the bird and problem-solving techniques used in modeling it? Was new vocabulary used during the presentation? | | • Are drawings accurate in color and shape? Detailed? Did students employ various drawing techniques? <br> • Is the bird's habitat well defined and correct? <br> • Do writings use new vocabulary to imaginatively express the bird's view from above? |
| | • Ask students to reflect on this lesson and write a DREAM statement to summarize the most important things they learned. | | |
| **Extensions** | Set up a bird feeder outside a classroom window. Mount pictures of native birds nearby and a chart for keeping track of sightings. Keep binoculars handy and encourage students to watch for birds during their free time and record their sightings on the chart. Take photographs for reference. <br><br> Younger children and some with special needs could sketch their bird before modeling to help them plan their use of color and form. | Children write short stories or poems about their birds to display with their sculptures. | Encourage older students to explore the Audubon Society Web site and participate in some of their activities. <br><br> Gifted children could choose two or three intriguing birds to research in depth, sculpt realistic models, and present to the group. Write a story from the viewpoint of one of the birds. |

**Hand-Carved Bluebird**
Artist: Tom Ahern
12" x 5" x 5"
Painted wood, driftwood, metal
Private Collection.

**Purple Rooster**
Artist: Miguel Rodriguez
12" x 8" x 4"
Paint on wood carving
Collection of Crayola.

# Extraordinary Fish Stories

## Objectives

Students (K-4) create richly colored fish on poles with age-appropriate descriptive words and sentences on the back of the fish. They demonstrate an understanding of structures and functions through the creation of their fish.

Students interpret and explain a secondary level of meaning in a story.

Students (5-6) illustrate and write a fish book and share their stories with an audience of younger children.

## Multiple Intelligences

| Interpersonal | Logical-mathematical |
|---|---|
| Linguistic | Spatial |

## National Standards

| *Grades K-6* **Visual Arts Standard #2** Using knowledge of structures and functions | *Grades K-2* **English Language Arts Standard #3** Students apply a wide range of strategies to comprehend, interpret, evaluate, and appreciate texts. They draw on their prior experience, their interactions with other readers and writers, their knowledge of word meaning and of other texts, their word identification strategies, and their understanding of textual features (e.g., sound-letter correspondence, sentence structure, context, graphics). |
|---|---|
| *Grades K-6* **Visual Arts Standard #3** Choosing and evaluating a range of subject matter, symbols, and ideas | *Grades K-6* **English Language Arts Standard #11** Students participate as knowledgeable, reflective, creative, and critical members of a variety of literacy communities. **English Language Arts Standard #12** Students use spoken, written, and visual language to accomplish their own purposes (e.g., for learning, enjoyment, persuasion, and the exchange of information). |

## Background Information

There are many types of fish with similar and different body parts; however some body parts are common to all fish. Most fish bodies have dorsal fins and caudal or tail fins, heads, eyes, gills, and mouths. Fish that live in tropical waters are often more colorful than fish that live in colder waters. In some cultures fish are highly valued symbols. In Japan the carp is associated with living a long life. Eating carp is thought to bring longevity to the diner. Some fish are known for strength because of their behaviors. Salmon, for instance, spawn every year and often struggle to return to areas to lay their eggs.

Often people who go fishing preserve their catch by having them mounted to display. Also, it is common for people who fish to tell tales about the big fish that got away.

## Resources

*A Field Guide to Freshwater Fishes: North America North of Mexico* by Brooks M. Burr and Lawrence M. Page
A Peterson field guide with illustrations and descriptions of fish for more advanced elementary students.

*Flotsam* by David Wiesner
A Caldecott winner, the seaside illustrations in this wordless picture book provide inspiration for student art.

*Making Books That Fly, Fold, Wrap, Hide, Pop Up, Twist, and Turn* by Gwen Diehn
Detailed directions for more than 18 different handmade books including pop-ups. Clear line drawings and full-color photographs of finished projects clarify directions. For older elementary students.

*Swimmy* by Leo Lionni
Undersea collage illustrations especially appeal to young children. All readers can understand the message about cooperation. Good introduction to literary themes for older readers.

*The Rainbow Fish* by Marcus Pfister
For young elementary students. Message about sharing is accessible to all readers. Illustrations include shiny, patterned scales.

## Vocabulary List

*Use this list to explore new vocabulary, create idea webs, or brainstorm related subjects.*

- Art vocabulary

| Collage | Pastels | Texture |
|---|---|---|
| Contrast | Pattern | Watercolor |
| Illustrations | | |

- Fish vocabulary

| Carp | Gills | Puffer |
|---|---|---|
| Fins | Hermit crab | Scales |
| Flotsam | Oceanography | Seahorse |

- Literary vocabulary

| Audience | Imagery | Resolution |
|---|---|---|
| Characters | Plot | Symbolism |
| Fantasy | Problem | Theme |

Artwork by students from
Alexander Elementary School, Houston, Texas.
Teacher: Marcy Muellar

## What Does It Mean?

**Collage:** art composed by attaching on a single surface various materials not typically associated with one another

**Structures:** the relationship or organization of the component parts of a work of art

**Visual symbols:** perception in the mind of a representation of a conventional, printed, or written figure

Artwork by students from
St. Theresa School,
Hellertown, Pennsylvania.

# Extraordinary Fish Stories

| | K-2 | 3-4 | 5-6 |
|---|---|---|---|
| **Suggested Preparation and Discussion** | Create a display of fish books and pictures as well as examples of the art projects students will make. Establish an aquarium of live fish if possible. Ask students to observe and compare various fish. Consider colors, markings, patterns, shape, size, and other characteristics. | | |
| | Read *The Rainbow Fish* or *Swimmy*. Ask children what they think the book is really about. Look at the illustrations. Discuss and use related vocabulary to talk about fish. | Share children's picture books about fish. Examine illustrations. | Review field guides that show various species of fish. Tell students they will create a book that illustrates a fish story. |
| **Crayola® Supplies** | • Oil Pastels  • School Glue | • Construction Paper™ Crayons • Watercolors | • Glitter Glue |
| | • Scissors | | |
| | | • Colored Pencils | |
| **Other Materials** | • Cotton swabs | • Recycled newspaper • Stapler and staples • Water containers | • Drawing paper • Glue-coated ribbon • Lined paper |
| | • Brown paper grocery bags  • Hole punch  • Yarn or string | | |
| **Set-up/Tips** | • Demonstrate how to cut fish from folded paper. • Show children how to blend oil pastels with fingertips or a cotton swab. | • Cover painting surface with newspaper. | • Attach glue-coated ribbon to book spine. |
| | • Demonstrate how to cut symmetrical fish from folded paper. | | |
| **Process: Session 1 20-30 min.** | **Create fish** 1. Fold drawing paper in half. Cut away from the fold to create a large fish. Open paper. 2. Make fins, tails, gills, and other body parts from cut-away scraps or draw directly on fish. 3. With oil pastels, create patterned designs on one side of the fish and the body parts. Glue body parts to fish. Air-dry the glue. 4. Cut a small hole for the fish mouth. Thread yarn through the hole and knot. | **Create and describe fish** 1. Open a paper grocery bag flat. Fold it in half. Cut away from the fold to create a fish. Open paper. 2. Draw fish features on one side. Decorate with fish features such as scales, eyes, mouth, and fins using Construction Paper Crayons. 3. Draw colored pencil lines on the back of the fish. With crayon, write simple sentences with descriptive words about the fish species. 4. Brush a watercolor wash over the crayon (crayon resist). Air-dry paint. | **Draft "fish story"** 1. Students identify one fish as the main character of their stories. Imagine a setting for the fish story and establish a problem. If there are other characters, what do they look like and what roles will they play? How will the problem be resolved? 2. Draft stories on lined paper, keeping a young audience in mind. Exchange drafts with other students to check for spelling, grammar, and story completeness. |

Fish Sculptures
Artist unknown
Paper, paint, wood
12" x 24" x 6"
Private Collection.

| | K-2 | 3-4 | 5-6 |
|---|---|---|---|
| **Process: Session 2** 20-30 min. | **Make fishing pole** 5. Cut a large rectangle from a paper grocery bag. Roll from the narrow end to create a tight cylinder. Glue edges. 6. Tie yarn from the fish to one end of pole. Glue yarn to pole. Air-dry the glue. | **Create 3-D fish and pole** 5. Fold the fish. Staple around the sides, leaving the head area open. 6. Crumple newspaper. Stuff the fish body to achieve a 3-D effect. Staple closed. 7. Create fishing pole (see K-2 Session 2). | **Illustrate book cover** 3. Fold drawing paper in half to form book cover. Cut out a fish shape using the fold as the binding of the book. 4. Decorate the book cover to reflect a species of fish. Add sparkle with Glitter Glue. Air-dry. |
| **Process: Session 3** 20-30 min. | **Write descriptions** 7. On plain side of the fish, write new vocabulary words around the outer edges. 8. In the middle, older students write sentences explaining what the story they read means. | **Share stories** 8. Students read sentences aloud to one another. Invite book buddies from a younger class to listen to the sentences. Read sentences with expression and energy. | **Assemble book** 5. Place fish shape on lined paper. Trace around fish. Cut out pages for the book. Neatly copy the edited story on the fish-shaped pages. 6. Insert the pages into the cover. Staple book together at tail. Cover binding with glue-coated ribbon. |
| **Process: Session 4** 20-30 min. | **Read** 9. Students exchange fish and read the words that appear on them. | | **Share story** 7. Students read stories aloud, with expression and energy, to each other. Add body and hand action to the storytelling activity. Invite book buddies from a younger class to listen to the stories. |
| **Assessment** | • Are fish designs richly textured and patterned? • Are fish assembled on the pole properly? • Are vocabulary words correctly spelled? | • Are 3-D fish constructed according to directions? Do words and sentences describe in detail the species of fish? • Are vocabulary words accurately spelled and neatly written? | • Are books properly designed and assembled? • Are stories written as directed? Are sentences complete? Do stories communicate to younger children? |
| | • Ask students to reflect on this lesson and write a DREAM statement to summarize the most important things they learned from their research and hands-on activity. | | |
| **Extensions** | Read other Leo Lionni books and discuss the messages. Assist younger children and some with special needs with knot tying. Store fishes and poles in a large box decorated like a tackle box. Advanced students write a fish story on the back of the fish. | Academically talented students research and report on several species of fish. Ask one or more people who fish to share their stories. | Encourage children with interest in fishing to share real fish stories with the class. Students research to compare the similarities and differences between two fish species. Report findings. Act out the stories. Create sets, costumes, and tickets. Perform for other children or school families. |
| | Visit an aquarium to observe shapes, colors, and behaviors of real fish. Make sketches. | | |

## Objectives

Students read fiction or nonfiction in which character development and setting are central to the text.

Students create their own painted papers, and then design, cut, and assemble collages inspired by the work of Henri Matisse and other graphic artists.

Students demonstrate an understanding of the connections between art and literature by using their collages to illustrate stories or poems authored by themselves or others.

## Multiple Intelligences

| Linguistic | Logical-mathematical |
| --- | --- |

## National Standards

| **Visual Arts Standard #1**<br>Understanding and applying media, techniques, and processes | **English Language Arts Standard #3**<br>Students apply a wide range of strategies to comprehend, interpret, evaluate and appreciate texts. They draw on their prior experience, their interactions with other readers and writers, their knowledge of word meaning and of other texts, their word identification strategies, and their understanding of textual features (e.g., sound-letter correspondence, sentence structure, context, graphics).<br><br>**English Language Arts Standard #7**<br>Students conduct research on issues and interest by generating ideas and questions, and by posing problems. They gather, evaluate, and synthesize data from a variety of sources (e.g., print and nonprint texts, artifacts, people) to communicate their discoveries in ways that suit their purpose and audience. |
| --- | --- |

## Background Information

The word *collage* comes from the French word *coller*, which means to *glue*. Collage is an art form in which bits of objects, such as newspaper, cloth, and pressed flowers are glued together to create a picture or incorporated into a traditional drawing or painting.

Picasso was one of the first modern artists to incorporate scraps of drawings and even news clippings into his paintings. The painter Matisse, when he was very old and ill, found that although he could no longer paint with brush on canvas, he was able to make colorful paper cutouts. Today these are among his best-loved works.

A sculptural collage made with three-dimensional objects is known by the French word *assemblage*.

## Resources

*Henri Matisse: Jazz* by Henri Matisse
Collection of vivid, abstract collages that is Matisse's visual response to the mood created by jazz. Handwritten text explains the significance of various colors and images. An especially good resource for teaching the concept of mood to older students. Can be used on varying levels with all ages.

*Matisse: Cut-Out Fun With Matisse* by Henri Matisse, Nina Hollein, and Max Hollein
Traces the development of Matisse's artistic style in a manner accessible to children of all ages. Illustrations, by Matisse himself, inspire readers to create their own collages.

*"Slowly, Slowly, Slowly," Said the Sloth* by Eric Carle
The delightfully verbal retort of a gentle, self-confident sloth that is criticized by other animals appeals to all readers. Detailed, colorful collages are a fine accompaniment to the text.

*The Great Ball Game: A Muskogee Story* retold by Joseph Bruchac
Native American story about a bat that shows opposing animals the way to peace. Includes fine collage illustrations. Good discussion starter for 8- and 9-year-olds but also appeals to younger children.

*Where the Sidewalk Ends* by Shel Silverstein
Book of poetry and humorous illustrations for children of all ages.

## Vocabulary List

*Use this list to explore new vocabulary,
create idea webs, or brainstorm related subjects.*

- Art vocabulary

| | | |
| --- | --- | --- |
| Abstract | Illustration | Overlap |
| Assemblage | Irregular | Pattern |
| Balance | Light | Shape |
| Collage | Movement | Texture |
| Composition | Organic | Unity |

- Literature vocabulary

| | | |
| --- | --- | --- |
| Character | Plot | Prose |
| Mood | Poetry | Setting |
| Narrative | | |

- *"Slowly, Slowly, Slowly," Said the Sloth* vocabulary

| | | |
| --- | --- | --- |
| Impassive | Mellow | Stoic |
| Lackadaisical | Placid | Tranquil |
| Languid | Slothful | Unflappable |
| Lethargic | Sluggish | |

## What Does It Mean?

**Abstract:** art that emphasizes line, color, and general or geometric forms and how they relate to one another

**Unified:** all the parts in a work are harmonious and appear to be complete, one area does not stand out over another

Artwork by students from Mt. Prospect Elementary School, Basking Ridge, New Jersey.
Teacher: Kamyee Ladas

| K-2 | 3-4 | 5-6 |
|---|---|---|
| Collect books with collage illustrations by artists such as Eric Carle, Ezra Jack Keats, Susan Roth, or Leo Lionni. Display reproductions of collage/assemblage work by Matisse and Picasso. Use all as inspiration for decorating paper and preparing collages. | | |
| Read *"Slowly, Slowly, Slowly," Said the Sloth* or a similar book. Discuss the story in terms of character and setting. Who is the main character? <br><br> What are some adjectives the other characters use to describe that character? How would you describe the character? Where does the story take place? | Read *The Great Ball Game* or similar material. Review characterization and setting. Introduce plot (What is the problem in the story?) and theme (What is the meaning behind the story?). | Share *Jazz* or another valuable work together. Review the elements of storytelling (plot, setting, characterization, and theme). Talk about how fine artists often use many of these same elements. <br><br> Introduce a fifth element: mood. What mood does Matisse seem to convey in *Jazz*? How does his use of color, shapes, and symbols help create mood and meaning? What techniques do poets use to create mood in literature? Read and discuss several sample poems. |

Examine book illustrations closely. Ask how children think the pictures were made. How do they help tell the story or set the mood? Talk about shapes, textures, and colors. What techniques and mediums can be used to create textures?

Explain that children will make their own decorated papers with which to cut and assemble collages. Matisse focused more on color and shape than detail with his collages, so avoid making papers too "busy" with design. Focus on color and simple texture, using watercolor washes, textured tempera, and mirror-painted papers. Several techniques from which to choose are described in Session 1.

**Suggested Preparation and Discussion**

# Cutting-Edge Collages: Character, Meaning, & Mood

|  | K-2 | 3-4 | 5-6 |
|---|---|---|---|
| Crayola® Supplies | • Colored Pencils  • Crayons  • Fingerpaint (optional)  • Glue  • Markers  • Model Magic® (optional)  • Paint Brushes  • Scissors  • Tempera Paint  • Watercolors  • White paper | | |
| Other Materials | • Construction paper  • Modeling tools such as craft sticks and plastic dinnerware  • Paper plates  • Paper towels  • Recycled newspaper  • Sponges, combs, and other texturing materials  • Water containers | | |
| Set-up/Tips | • Cover painting surface with newspaper. | | |

**Process: Session 1**
**30-40 min.**

**Create decorative papers**

1. Create several papers using at least two of these techniques.

   **Mirror-Image Painted Paper:** Fold paper in half and open. Place a tablespoon each of two or three colors of tempera in the center. Refold paper gently. Smooth with fingers to spread paint inside paper. Open fold to reveal colorful design.

   **Watercolor Washes:** Apply watercolor washes to wet white paper. Experiment with mixing and bleeding colors. Sponge-paint dark colors over light ones that have air-dried.

   **Textured Paper:** Mix opaque tempera to create unique colors. Apply to papers with brushes, sponges, combs, or other materials.

   **Textured Crayon:** Lay textured objects under paper. Rub the side of an unwrapped crayon across the top of the paper. For crayon resist, top the texture with paint. The crayon wax will resist the paint.

   **Fingerpainted Paper:** Sprinkle water on fingerpaint paper. Spread paint to coat paper evenly. Draw in paint with fingers, recycled comb, or other tools.

   **Stamped Paper:** To make a stamp, roll a ping-pong ball-sized Model Magic sphere. Pinch top to create a handle. Make designs on the bottom of the stamp by pressing it against a textured surface or by etching it with modeling tools. Air-dry at least 24 hours. Place a clean, damp sponge on a paper plate. Spread 3 or 4 tablespoons of tempera on the sponge. Dab stamp on sponge. Press stamp onto paper to create patterns.

   Air-dry all painted papers flat.

---

**Process: Session 2**

**Grades K-2**
**30-45 min.**

**Grades 3-6**
**45-60 min.**

| **Create collages** | **Write poems** | **Write short story** |
|---|---|---|
| 2. Children cut the character from decorated papers. Encourage them to use different papers for various parts. <br> 3. Cut out other objects to show the setting, such as trees or furniture. | 2. Each student researches a poetry example and then writes a poem to share with others. | 2. Research and review stories written by various authors. Students write short stories to describe a person in a setting and involved in an activity. |

---

**Process: Session 3**

**Grades K-2**
**30-45 min.**

**Grades 3-4**
**45-60 min.**

**Grade 5-6**
**45-60 min.**

| | **Create collages** | **Create collages and assemble anthology** |
|---|---|---|
| 4. Lay pieces on construction paper. Experiment with arrangements to achieve a balanced, unified picture. Some pieces may overlap. Glue all pieces down. <br> 5. Add details such as eyes, nose, tail, or ears with markers. | 3. Sketch a collage design first. What symbols, colors, and shapes will help convey the mood and meaning of the poem? <br> 4. Cut shapes from the decorated papers. Place them on a construction paper background. <br> 5. Experiment with various layouts to find one that creates the mood of the poetry and is aesthetically pleasing in the space. Glue pieces into place. | 3. Sketch a collage design that is aligned to the story. What symbols, colors, and shapes help convey the mood and meaning of the story? <br> 4. Cut shapes from the decorated papers. Place them on a construction paper background. Experiment with various layouts to find one that creates the mood of the story and is aesthetically pleasing in the space. Glue pieces into place. <br> 5. Assemble the stories into a class anthology with a decorated cover. |

| | K-2 | 3-4 | 5-6 |
|---|---|---|---|
| **Assessment** | • Did each student use several different techniques to decorate papers? Are colors varied? Is there evidence of texturing?<br>• Are multiple pieces of paper combined to create the collage images?<br>• Ask students to reflect on this lesson and write a DREAM statement to summarize the most important things they learned. | | |
| | • Does the collage include a story character?<br>• Are character features included in the collage? | • Does the collage illustrate a specific poem? Is there an attempt to recreate the poem's mood through the use of color, shape, line, and light?<br>• Has the artist paid attention to all space on the page? | • Ask students to take turns reading their stories to the class. Challenge listeners to check that the story makes sense and has a beginning, middle, and end. Students show their collage illustration to check to see if the design matches the story text.<br>• Have all students contributed to creating a class story anthology? |
| **Extensions** | Encourage students to describe the character they created. Use descriptive language. Some may prefer to write the description while others may choose to tell it.<br><br>Especially young students or those with special needs may have difficulty with cutting. Some may prefer to cut directly into the paper. Others may wish to draw the shapes and then cut. A few may need assistance. Others may prefer to tear the paper, which also creates an interesting edge effect. | Mix up the art and poems. Children match each other's collages to the poetry that inspired the art. Analyze the attributes that led to their selections.<br><br>Hold a Poetry Festival. Display collages and invite the student artists to read or recite the accompanying poems. Audience could be classmates, another class, families, or community visitors.<br><br>Children with strong research skills could gather information on a subject, while more artistic students could create sample projects, and good speakers could give a talk on the subject. | Invite book authors and illustrators to share their work with the class.<br><br>Create anthologies that focus on specific topics. Publish multiple copies.<br><br>Research collage artists and make oral reports to the class. |

Group students with varying skills to explore and research other types of paper cutting. Chinese Paper Cutting is an intricate art form that dates back to the 6th century. Japanese Kirigami and the German/Swiss Scherenschnitte are two other forms of that folk art. The latter was popularized in the United States by German immigrants known as the Pennsylvania Dutch.

Provide left-handed scissors for students who need them.

Investigate and invent new ways to make decorative papers.

Paris Collage
Artist R. De Long
Paper, glue, ribbon, foil
12" x 16"
Private Collection.

Artwork by students from
Sunflower Elementary School,
Lenexa, Kansas.
Teacher: Rosie Riordan

**Crayola** **Dream~Makers**
Building fun and creativity into standards-based learning

# Illuminate Your Letters!

## Objectives

Students create illuminated letters modeled after medieval illuminated manuscripts.

Students (K-4) use the writing process to practice and legibly write letters to family or friends using their best penmanship.

Students (5-6) research and compare typefaces to use as the basis for inventing a new font.

## Multiple Intelligences

Interpersonal
Linguistic
Spatial

## What Does It Mean?

**Font:** style of typeface or lettering

**Illuminate:** make resplendent by decorating letters, pages, paragraphs, or borders with colors and gold or silver as was done in the Middle Ages

**Vellum:** calfskin, lambskin, or other materials treated to use as writing surface. Manuscripts in the Middle Ages were often made using vellum pages with leather book covers and bindings.

## National Standards

**Visual Arts Standard #3**
Choosing and evaluating a range of subject matter, symbols and ideas

**Visual Arts Standard #4**
Understanding the visual arts in relation to history and cultures

**English Language Arts Standard #4**
Students adjust their use of spoken, written and visual language (e.g., conventions, style, vocabulary) to communicate effectively with a variety of audiences and for different purposes.

**English Language Arts Standard #5**
Students employ a wide range of strategies as they write and use different writing process elements appropriately to communicate with different audiences for a variety of purposes.

## Background Information

Letter writing has a long history. In medieval times commoners were often illiterate and hired scribes to write letters for them when necessary. Historically, letters offer a glimpse into the lives of ordinary people. For example, Duke University's Special Collections Library includes original letters and diaries written by women during the Civil War. Texts of some, including the diary of a 10-year-old girl, are available on line at library.duke.edu/specialcollections/bingham.

The National Postal Museum in Washington, D.C., also holds several collections of letters including more than 75 that are woven throughout the museum's galleries to personalize the exhibits. Today, e-mail is changing the art of letter writing yet again.

## Resources

*Catherine Called Birdy* by Karen Cushman
Novel for older elementary/middle school students. Fictionalized journal of a young medieval girl. Each entry begins with an illuminated letter.

*Dear Mr. Henshaw* by Beverly Cleary
Through letters to a favorite author, a third-grade boy reflects on life and learns to deal with difficult family circumstances.

*Gone Wild: An Endangered Animal Alphabet* by David McLimans
A 2007 Caldecott Honor Book and fine example of graphic design. Focuses on both illuminated letters and endangered animals. Excellent inspiration for art students of any age.

*Illuminate Letters* by Stephan Oliver
Illustrated reference of materials and step-by-step illumination processes. A good teacher reference.

*Masterpieces of Illuminated Letters and Borders* by W.P. Tymms and M.D. Wyatt
Numerous embellished letters and decorative designs from medieval manuscripts. Inspires students' illuminations.

*The Illuminated Alphabet* by Timothy Noad and Patricia Seligman
Step-by-step guide to create an illuminated manuscript. For teacher reference.

## Vocabulary List

*Use this list to explore new vocabulary, create idea webs, or brainstorm related subjects.*

- Letters
  - Alphabetical
  - Capital
  - Print
  - Script
  - Symbols

- Letter writing
  - Closing
  - Comma
  - Correspondence
  - Envelope
  - Greeting
  - Heading
  - Inside address
  - Letterhead
  - Signature
  - ZIP code

- Middle Ages
  - Cloisters
  - Gold leaf
  - Illuminations
  - Manuscript
  - Medieval
  - Monastery
  - Monk
  - Parchment
  - Scribe
  - Vellum

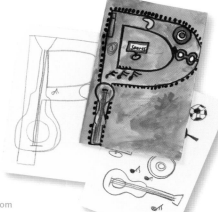

Artwork by students from St. Theresa School, Hellertown, Pennsylvania.

Ms. Annie Fannie
83 Lovely Blossom
Lane
Taipei, Taiwan
April 22nd, 2007

Dear Annie,

How are you? I hope you're doing fine in Taiwan. I am! We finished the NJASK a couple of weeks ago. Boy, am I glad! Now I can relax.

Have you ever heard of Unicef? If you haven't, it's an organization which helps poor or needy people. Right now were having something called the Chore-a-Thon, to raise money for Unicef. We have to do chores, sell things, etc. to earn money to donate. Amy sells candy, gum, and origami, and she's raised more money than I've made so far. Do you have ideas?

For spring break, I went to India, and it was a fun experience. I went to two different cities. There is lots of my family there. My favorite part was going to an amusement park. There were many water rides and land rides. Some even went upside-down! There, the weather is always warm. Is it cold in Taiwan? It's mixed in America, which is what I like.

See you in the summer! I can't wait until you visit!
Sincerely,
Brenda

Crayola
Dream~Makers
Building fun and creativity into standards-based learning

# Illuminate Your Letters!

| | K-2 | 3-4 | 5-6 |
|---|---|---|---|
| **Suggested Preparation and Discussion** | Display as appropriate to students' ages and abilities:<br>• diagram of formal letter format<br>• illuminated letter styles from various historic periods<br>• alphabet books, especially those with illuminated letters<br>• collections of letters and stories told through letter writing<br>• sample art projects with illuminated letters | | |
| | Examine alphabet books. Talk about personal initials. Strengthen phonemic awareness by making lists of words that start with the same letter/beginning sound. Make sound-letter associations.<br><br>Children draft short, friendly letters to a family member or friend. Check spelling. Use complete sentences that communicate a message. Use proper writing conventions. | Discuss the role monks and scribes played in the history of writing during medieval times. Talk about reasons for letter writing and the use of letterhead and illuminated stationery. Read selections from novels that reflect the medieval period and/or the use of letter writing to tell a story.<br><br>Review proper letter-writing format. Discuss differences between a business letter and a friendly letter. After reading selections from letter collections, each student drafts a friendly letter to a friend or family member with a particular purpose in mind. Do they wish to inform, persuade, or convey emotion? | Examine various styles of illuminated lettering and contemporary fonts found on computers. Research and discuss the history of fonts and typefaces. |
| **Crayola® Supplies** | • Crayons | • Markers | • Watercolor Colored Pencils |
| | • Glue   • Scissors   • Tempera Paints (black and Premier™ gold) | | |
| | • Paint Brushes | | |
| **Other Materials** | • Brown paper grocery bags   • Envelopes, #10 white | | • Rulers |
| | • Lined paper   • Paper towels<br>• Postage stamps<br>• Recycled newspaper<br>• Water containers | • White paper | |
| | • Paper towels   • Recycled newspaper   • Water containers | | |
| **Set-up/Tips** | • Cover painting surface with newspaper. | | |
| **Process: Session 1 10-15 min.** | **Create "antique" paper**<br>1. Cut a 6-inch square from a brown grocery bag. Crumple it slightly. Dip it in water, squeeze out water, and lay flat.<br>2. Brush on black tempera. Leave paint on for 3 to 4 minutes. Rinse painted paper in clean water to remove surface paint. Leave paint in crumpled areas. Air-dry flat. | **Create "vellum-like" papers**<br>1. Stain several sheets of white drawing paper with thinned tempera paint. Tear the edges so the paper takes on an aged look. Flatten papers using recycled telephone books. Air-dry papers. | **Research fonts and typefaces**<br>1. Ask student to collect at least five completely distinct fonts. List similarities and differences. |

Illuminated Manuscript
Artist unknown
6" x 6"
Collection of Hannah Willett.

| | K-2 | 3-4 | 5-6 |
|---|---|---|---|
| **Process: Session 2** 15-20 min. | **Illuminate an initial** 3. Students write one of their initials in bubble-style letters on the antique paper. 4. Paint the letter with gold tempera. Air-dry flat. | **Illuminate an initial** 2. Students each select an illumination style. Outline an initial in that manner on the antique paper. 3. Paint the interior of the letter in gold. Air-dry flat. | **Create "guideline" papers** 2. Draw guidelines on several sheets of paper for use in developing a new upper- and lower-case typeface. |
| **Process: Session 3** 30-40 min. | **Finish friendly letters** 5. Outline initials with dark crayon. Fill surrounding areas with shapes and patterns to create an illuminated design. Glue the illuminated letter to lined writing paper. 6. Copy the friendly letter on the letterhead. | **Complete friendly letters** 4. Fill in the background with richly colored shapes, patterns, and images reminiscent of early illuminated texts. 5. Glue the illuminated letter to paper to create unique letterhead. 6. Copy friendly letters on letterhead, using proper format and correct spellings. | **Invent a font** 3. On one sheet of guideline paper, invent a font that combines several features in the typefaces collected. 4. Refine the font so it can be created in both upper and lower case. 5. Create the entire upper- and lower-case alphabet in the new font. |
| | **Prepare envelopes** 7. Decorate envelopes to match the style of the letterhead. 8. Fold letters and place in envelopes. Address, stamp, and mail letters. | | **Illuminate a font** 6. Choose at least one upper-case letter to illuminate. Dip watercolor pencils in water and/or brush to achieve illuminated effects. Air-dry illuminations. |
| **Assessment** | • Is the illuminated letter easily recognizable? Does it represent the child's own name? Is the space around the letter filled with shapes and colors that create a pleasing design? • Is the letter written in complete sentences? Are conventions of language appropriate for the ages and ability levels of the children? | • Does the illumination demonstrate an understanding of the concept of illuminated letters? • Is the letter clearly recognizable? Has the area around it been completely filled with colors and designs reminiscent of medieval manuscripts? • Does the written text convey a specific message using proper letter-writing format? | • Does the project reflect a familiarity with at least five contemporary fonts? • Has attention been paid to uniform details in the development of both upper- and lower-case letters in the font or typeface? • Is the work legible? • Does the illuminated letter embellish the new font and still leave it recognizable? |
| | • Are envelopes decorated in a manner consistent with the letterhead? | | |
| | • Ask students to reflect on this lesson and write a DREAM statement to summarize the most important things they learned in the lesson. | | |
| **Extensions** | Use standard lettering rather than an embellished style for students who are just beginning to master letter formation. Outlining and coloring letters reinforces learning. Some students with motor challenges may need to work with a scribe or computer to prepare the letterhead and/or write the letter. | Encourage interested students to make illuminated pages for alphabet books to share with younger children. Suggest that students create their own letterhead or calling card logos on the computer. Embellish with markers. Advanced students read excerpts from historic letters as an example of primary resource material. Compose imaginary letters to people who lived in the past. Encourage cooperative editing, especially to assist students with special needs. Look up fonts on the computer and embellish them. | |
| | Share excerpts from *The Jolly Postman: Other People's Letters* by Janet and Allan Ahlberg to inspire creative writing. Reflect on the letter-writing process and its results. What were the recipients' responses to getting the hand-made letters? Organize a pen pal program. | | Create a poster that lists classroom rules or notices using the new fonts. |

Crayola **Dream~Makers**
Building fun and creativity into standards-based learning

# Making Wishes and Dancing by Moonlight

## Objectives

Students read Amy Tan's *The Moon Lady* or a similar collection of Asian folktales and select one character (or its wish) to represent visually.

Students create expressive puppets with moveable limbs as inspired by their reading. Grades 5-6 make shadow puppets.

Students use their puppets in a theatrical setting to demonstrate the character and/or its wish.

## Multiple Intelligences

| | |
|---|---|
| Bodily-kinesthetic | Linguistic |
| Interpersonal | Spatial |
| Intrapersonal | |

## National Standards

| | |
|---|---|
| **Visual Arts Standard #1**<br>Understanding and applying media, techniques, and processes<br>**Visual Arts Standard #4**<br>Understanding the visual arts in relation to history and cultures<br>**Visual Arts Standard #6**<br>Making connections between visual arts and other disciplines | **English Language Arts Standard #4**<br>Students adjust their use of spoken, written, and visual language (e.g., conventions, style, vocabulary) to communicate effectively with a variety of audiences and for different purposes.<br>**English Language Arts Standard #9**<br>Students develop an understanding of and respect for diversity in language use, patterns and dialects across cultures, ethnic groups, geographic regions, and social roles.<br>**English Language Arts Standard #11**<br>Students participate as knowledgeable, reflective, creative, and critical members of a variety of literacy communities.<br>**English Language Arts Standard #12**<br>Students use spoken, written, and visual language to accomplish their own purposes (e.g., for learning, enjoyment, persuasion, and the exchange of information). |

## Background Information

Indonesian shadow puppets have been used by the people of Java for more than 1,000 years. The bodies, heads, and arms of the puppets are meticulously created out of leather and then painted. The handle that is used to hold the puppet in place is created out of a very hard ebony wood. Shadow puppets are held up to a translucent screen which is lit from behind so the puppets cast shadows on the screen. Puppeteers move the arms and the bodies of these puppets to tell stories that convey messages of love, hope, and everyday life.

## Resources

*Art from Many Hands: Multicultural Art Projects*
by Jo Miles Schuman
Resource for both art and classroom teachers. Includes projects for elementary and middle school students as well as cultural information. One section is devoted to Asian arts.

*Children of the Dragon: Selected Stories From Vietnam*
by Sherry Garland
Filled with unforgettable characters and vividly detailed Vietnamese settings. Collection includes the story of Chu Cuai, a favorite tale often told during the Moon Festival.

*Making Shadow Puppets* by Jill Bryant and Catherine Heard
Creative inspiration and directions for elementary students.

*The Moon Lady* by Amy Tan
Told by a Chinese grandmother to her three American grand-daughters, this is a story from her own childhood about the night she saw the Moon Lady in a shadow play and learned a valuable lesson about wishes.

*Tongues of Jade* by Laurence Yep
Collection of Chinese folktales for older elementary and middle school students. A broad background in Chinese cultural beliefs and traditions.

## Vocabulary List

*Use this list to explore new vocabulary,*
*create idea webs, or brainstorm related subjects.*

Courtyard
Dalang
Dragonfly
Eel
Expressive
Fables
Festival
Form
Gamelan
Illusion
Incense
Jade
Jasmine
Kulit
Longevity
Lotus
Mah-Jongg
Mooncake
Moongate

Nai-Nai
Opaque
Proportion
Puppeteer
Representational
Rickshaw
Shadow puppet
Shape
Sundial
Symbol/symbolic
Teahouse
Texture
Waywang
Ying-Yang

Artwork by students from South Mountain Middle School, Allentown, Pennsylvania. Teacher: Shari Kaucher

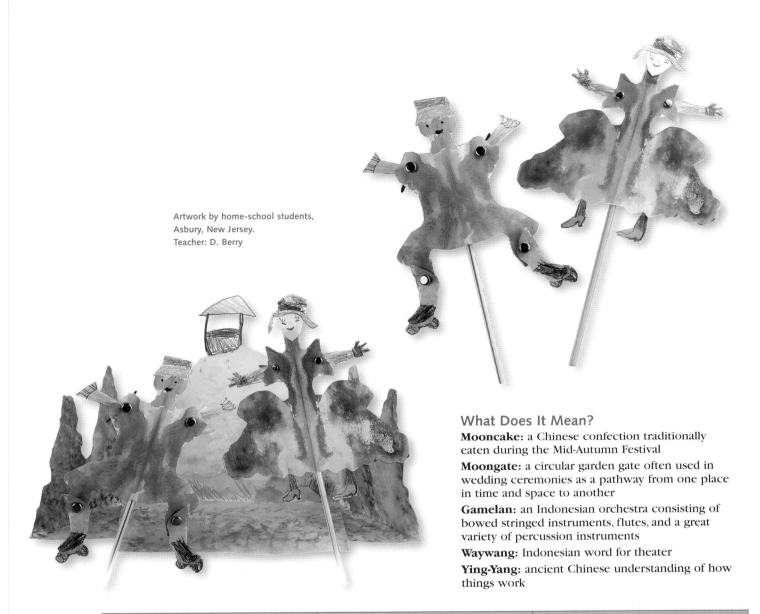

Artwork by home-school students,
Asbury, New Jersey.
Teacher: D. Berry

## What Does It Mean?

**Mooncake:** a Chinese confection traditionally eaten during the Mid-Autumn Festival

**Moongate:** a circular garden gate often used in wedding ceremonies as a pathway from one place in time and space to another

**Gamelan:** an Indonesian orchestra consisting of bowed stringed instruments, flutes, and a great variety of percussion instruments

**Waywang:** Indonesian word for theater

**Ying-Yang:** ancient Chinese understanding of how things work

| | K-2 | 3-4 | 5-6 |
|---|---|---|---|
| **Suggested Preparation and Discussion** | Display a variety of books and materials related to Asian culture and puppetry. Include a few sample handmade shadow puppets. <br><br> Discuss major Asian festivals such as the Moon Festival and Chinese New Year as well as the role storytelling plays in these events. <br><br> If any students know how to make hand-shadow puppets, ask them to demonstrate. Then show how one of the shadow puppets from the display works. Compare different types of puppets such as stick puppets, finger puppets, and hand puppets. | | |
| | Read aloud an Asian folktale appropriate to the ages and ability levels of students. Ask students to visualize the characters and select one to recreate as a shadow puppet. If *The Moon Lady* was read, have children think of a wish they might make and choose a visual symbol to represent that wish. Give several examples and discuss ideas. | | Read a variety of Asian folktales together and/or independently. Form small groups to select a tale to dramatize with shadow puppets. Students review their stories and select characters for which to make puppets. |

Crayola **Dream-Makers**
Building fun and creativity into standards-based learning

# Making Wishes and Dancing by Moonlight

|  | K-2 | 3-4 | 5-6 |
|---|---|---|---|
| **Crayola® Supplies** | • Colored Pencils  • Markers<br>• Paint Brushes  • School Glue<br>• Tempera Paint | • Tempera Paint (optional)<br>• Watercolors | • Markers |
|  | • Scissors | | |
| **Other Materials** | • Construction paper<br>• Drawing paper<br>• Overhead projector or spotlight<br>• Paper towels<br>• Recycled newspaper<br>• Water containers<br>• Watercolor paper | • Plastic drinking straws<br>• Watercolor paper | • Bed sheet (clean, plain, light colored)<br>• Clear adhesive tape<br>• Dowel sticks  • Hole punch<br>• Masking tape  • Poster board<br>• Spotlight  • Tracing paper |
|  |  | • Brass paper fasteners | |
| **Set-up/Tips** | • Students set up the presentation area/theater ahead of time so they can experiment with their puppets as they create them.<br>• Cover painting area with newspaper. | | |
| **Process: Session 1 30-45 min.** | **Create textured paper**<br>1. Fold watercolor paper in half. Squeeze about 2 tablespoons of tempera paint (can combine colors) onto the middle.<br>2. Fold paper closed and smooth paint inside, being careful not to let the paint ooze out. Open paper. Air-dry flat.<br>**Form puppet handle**<br>3. Lay construction paper flat. Roll paper from the long side into a tight tube. Glue. Press edge until secure. Air-dry.<br>4. Decorate handle with markers.<br>5. Gently flatten the handle. Draw vertical designs up and down the handle and horizontal designs on the back and front of cylinder. | **Create puppet papers**<br>1. Sketch ideas for updated hair styles, clothing, scenes, and accessories for characters on paper.<br>2. Fold drawing paper in half to begin a symmetrical fold painting that will serve as the character's body trunk.<br>3. Open paper. Drop various colors of juicy watercolor or washable paint on one side of fold. Colors should help communicate the puppet's character.<br>4. Fold sides together. Rub over the outside of the unpainted side to transfer the paint.<br>5. Open and observe the mirror effect. Add more paint and repeat process as needed for more detail or to change image.<br>6. Decorate additional papers using the same paint technique for body parts and stage sets. Air-dry the painted papers. | **Make shadow puppets**<br>1. Outline puppet characters on poster board, paying attention to form and proportion. Cut out shapes.<br>2. To make jointed puppets, cut arms, legs, wings, and other parts separately. Punch holes and loosely attach to puppet's body with brass paper fasteners.<br>3. Sketch interior details (eyes, nose, scales, fins, feathers for animals; facial features and clothing for people). Cut out interior shapes.<br>4. Cover the openings with small pieces of tracing paper. Tape in place. Color tracing paper with markers.<br>5. Paint puppets with watercolors. Air-dry paint. |

Artwork by students from Tanglewood Elementary School, Fort Worth, Texas. Teacher: Jessica Patterson

|  | K-2 | 3-4 | 5-6 |
|---|---|---|---|
| **Process:**<br>**Session 2**<br>**20-30 min.** | 6. Place the puppet flat on drawing paper. Draw around it, leaving a 1-inch border. Write words describing the character or wish in the margin.<br><br>7. Glue the handle to the top of the outline. Place the back of the puppet on the handle. Glue it, so the handle is sandwiched in the middle. Air-dry the glue. | 7. Cut out body parts and assemble with brass fasteners. Fold, cut out and glue the stage following the diagram. | **Prepare the stage and rehearse**<br>6. Hang a sheet over two chairs or an overhead rod. Place a spotlight on a table several feet behind it.<br><br>7. Students kneel out of the line of the spotlight, behind the curtain, and practice working their puppets while retelling their tales. |

<table>
<tr><td>Process:<br>Session 3<br>20-30 min.</td><td>Present puppets<br>8. Take turns presenting puppets to the class. For those with "wish" puppets, classmates try to identify wishes from puppets' shapes and verbal clues. Those with character puppets re-enact portions of the story.</td><td colspan="2">Perform the play<br>8. Student groups take turns performing puppet shows for classmates. Enlist a "reader" for any students who find it difficult to work the puppet and deliver lines at the same time. Lines can also be written on the backs of the puppets.</td></tr>
<tr><td rowspan="2">Assessment</td><td>• Can students explain differences between types of puppets?</td><td colspan="2">• Are puppets representative of the characters in the story in terms of form, line, color, and definitive details?<br>• Did students work collaboratively to select a tale, choose the characters, make the puppets, and present their show?</td></tr>
<tr><td colspan="3">• Did students create puppets representative of their wishes or characters from a specific folktale using the materials provided? Did students follow directions to create their puppets?<br>• Did they use the puppets effectively to demonstrate their wishes or retell the folktale?<br>• Ask students to reflect on this lesson and write a DREAM statement to summarize the most important things they learned.</td></tr>
<tr><td>Extensions</td><td>Celebrate the Moon Festival or Chinese New Year with students. Eat with chopsticks and serve traditional Chinese foods.<br><br>Some students with motor challenges may need assistance to prepare their textured papers and tear or cut out their puppets.</td><td colspan="2">Invite an audience of younger students to see the plays, or perform them for parents or the community.<br>Collaborate with a music specialist to add authentic Gamelan music to the performance.<br>Explore more about Javanese Waywangs with gifted students. Attend performances if possible. Listen to Gamelan music.<br>Create a more elaborate stage for the performance.</td></tr>
</table>

**Shadow Puppet**
Circa 1900s
Artist unknown
Hand painted and cut leather with ebony handles
27 3/4" x 21"
Indonesia
Private Collection.

——— = Cut
- - - - = Fold

**Paper Stage Setting**

Step 1.

Step 2.

Glue          Glue

# Beyond a Magic Dragon

## Objectives

Students respond to literary selections by discussing and analyzing themes and writing reflective solutions to bullying.

Student research and identify the impact of negative behavior they observe and that exists in popular culture and create a class display with mobiles (grades K-2), puppets (3-4), or a mural (5-6) that illustrate strategies to reverse these negative behaviors.

## Multiple Intelligences

Interpersonal
Intrapersonal
Linguistic

## What Does It Mean?

**Accordion-style fold:** folding paper pleats so the paper springs open and closed

**Horizontal:** a position that is parallel to the horizon, running across from side to side

**Vertical:** a position that is perpendicular to the horizon, going up and down

## National Standards

| Visual Arts Standard #3 | English Language Arts Standard #2 |
|---|---|
| Choosing and evaluating a range of subject matter, symbols, and ideas | Students read a wide range of literature from many periods in many genres t o build an understanding of the many dimensions (e.g., philosophical, ethical, aesthetic) of human experience. |
| | **English Language Arts Standard #7** |
| | Students conduct research on issues and interests by generating ideas and questions, and by posing problems. They gather, evaluate and synthesize data from a variety of sources (e.g., print and non-print texts, artifacts, people) to communicate their discoveries in ways that suit their purpose and audience. |

## Background Information

A bully is like an annoying dragon that is always breathing fire. A bully may be someone who hurts, frightens, or tyrannizes those who are smaller or weaker. Bullies might attack others with nasty actions, call people names, or even physically hurt victims. A bully can be a boy or a girl, young or grown up. Bullies often act out because they themselves fear people, places, and things and because they crave attention.

When people stand up against bullies in appropriate ways and offer peaceful solutions to life's puzzling situations, often the culture of a group changes. People can grow up, with their respect of self and others intact, to become fine citizens and peacemakers in their hearts.

## Resources

*Bullies Are a Pain in the Brain* by Trevor Romain
For middle and older elementary students, a self-help guide to dealing with bullies. Offers clear, helpful advice. Includes cartoon-style illustrations and a list of resources.

*Chrysanthemum* by Kevin Henkes
Young children struggling with social conflicts will empathize with Chrysanthemum, a mouse who is the victim of merciless teasing because of her unusual name. Gentle, reassuring illustrations.

*Stepping on the Cracks* by Mary Downing Hahn
Two friends gain insight into reasons behind bullying in this novel set during World War II. Inspires thoughtful discussion of complicated issues among older elementary students.

*The Book of Dragons* by Michael Hague
Diverse collection of dragon tales that has something for all ages. Vibrant and varied illustrations add to the appeal.

## Vocabulary List

*Use this list to explore new vocabulary, create idea webs, or brainstorm related subjects.*

Abuse
Aggressive
Assertive
Bully/bullying
Collaborate
Compassion
Conflict
Confrontation
Degrade
Demean
Discrimination
Empathy
Eye contact
Feelings
Humiliate
Image
Mediator
Moods
Patterns
Peacemaker
Peers
Persuasive
Resolution
Self-esteem
Shapes
Texture
Understanding
Victim

Artwork by students from St. Theresa School, Hellertown, Pennsylvania.

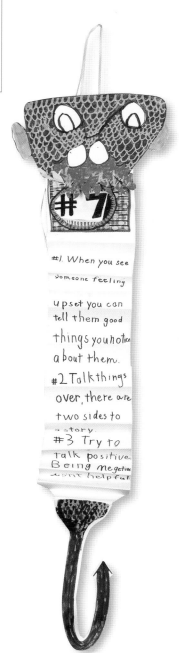

Artwork created by students from St. Theresa School, Hellertown, Pennsylvania.

#2 Talk things over
#3 Asking them to Politely stop

# 8

Artwork by students from Alexander Elementary School, Houston, Texas.
Teacher: Marcy Muellar

Crayola **Dream~Makers**
Building fun and creativity into standards-based learning

# Beyond a Magic Dragon

| | K-2 | 3-4 | 5-6 |
|---|---|---|---|
| **Suggested Preparation and Discussion** | Read and discuss a suitable children's story about bullying. Encourage students to share examples from their own lives or what they know from popular culture. What is a bully? How do you feel when you are bullied? How can you respond? Why do you think some people are bullies? What can we each do to help people get along and prevent bullying?<br><br>What is a dragon? In what ways are dragons sometimes like bullies? What does a dragon look like? What colors, shapes, or features might make it look angry or threatening? Use adjectives, adverbs, and other expressive language.<br><br>Explain that students will make mobiles, dragon puppets, and/or murals to represent bullies and will be asked to suggest solutions to the bullying problem.<br><br>Display a variety of dragon pictures from various cultures as well as examples of the craft. | | |
| **Crayola® Supplies** | • Colored Pencils • Markers • Scissors • School Glue | | |
| | | | • Paint Brushes • Tempera Paint |
| **Other Materials** | • Poster board • Ribbon | • Construction paper | • Mural paper • Paper towels<br>• Recycled newspaper<br>• Water containers |
| | • White drawing paper | | |
| **Set-up/Tips** | | • Roll the handle cylinders as tightly as possible. | • Cover painting surface with newspaper. |

**Storm Dragon Sculpture**
Artist: Scott Atiyeh
Air-dry clay
18" x 18" x 24"
Collection of Crayola.

**Dragon Scarf**
Artist unknown
Marker on silk
18" x 18"
Private Collection.

| | K-2 | 3-4 | 5-6 |
|---|---|---|---|
| **Process: Session 1**<br><br>Grades K-2<br>20-30 min.<br><br>Grades 3-4<br>5-10 min.<br><br>Grade 5-6<br>30-45 min.<br>or more | **Create a "How to Spot a Bully" class poster**<br>1. Brainstorm a list of behaviors that identify a bully.<br>2. Create class posters that list characteristics observed in bullies.<br>3. Embellish and decorate the borders with shapes and colors. Display posters.<br>4. Glue two sheets of drawing paper together end to end. Air-dry the glue. | **Design two puppet handles**<br>1. Lay construction paper flat. Roll paper from the long side into a tight tube. Glue. Press edge until secure. Make a second handle the same way. Air-dry glue. | **Create class dragon murals**<br>1. Paint a large dragon on mural paper. Leave the dragon mouth free of paint. Air-dry the paint. |
| **Process: Session 2**<br>30-45 min. | **Create a dragon mobile**<br>5. Write one or more bullying solutions on the glued paper. Fold them accordion style.<br>6. Draw and decorate a dragon head and tail, each on a separate paper. Cut them out.<br>7. Glue the dragon head to one end of the accordion fold. Glue the dragon tail to the opposite end.<br>8. Attach ribbon or sting to the dragon head to suspend. | **Create the puppet**<br>2. Decorate handles.<br>3. Draw a dragon to cover most of a large sheet of drawing paper. Include head, body, and tail.<br>4. Color the head and tail areas so they reflect features of a dragon. In body area, write at least one solution to bullying.<br>5. Accordion-fold the dragon. Glue handles to the dragon's head and tail. | **Create dragon flames with solution**<br>2. Reflect on research findings about solutions to bullying.<br>3. Cut out construction paper flames shapes. Write solutions to bullying on flames. Glue to mouth area on dragon mural. |
| **Process: Session 3**<br>30-45 min. | **Reflect on solutions to bullying**<br>9. Identify one or more of a bully's aggressive moods and feelings in class. Discuss how class solutions result in conflict resolution to solve negative behaviors. | | |
| **Assessment** | • Have students used color, texture, shape, and line, as well as expressive features to symbolize aggressive, bullying behaviors?<br>• Do words, phrases, and/or sentences written on dragon projects suggest thoughtful, positive solutions to bullying behaviors?<br>• Ask students to reflect on this lesson and write a DREAM statement to summarize the most important things they learned. | | |
| **Extensions** | Encourage students to discuss their use of color, shape, and design to symbolize bullying behaviors and/or their own feelings. Compare/contrast classmates' dragon projects.<br><br>Post key words in the classroom as a resource for students when they write their solutions to bullying. Provide word processors for students with special needs to use when generating their solutions. Recruit parent volunteers to help beginning writers translate their ideas into simple sentences.<br><br>Encourage advanced or gifted students to explore the concept of point of view by creating short stories or skits with contrasting viewpoints: the bully's as well as the victim's.<br><br>Cut out articles and images from magazines and newspapers that highlight specific incidences of negative behaviors in popular culture. Hold a class symposium that results in solutions to some of these incidences.<br><br>Plan an all-school assembly on conflict resolution.<br><br>Role-play solutions to bullying. | | |

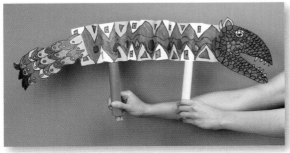

Artwork by students from
Mount Prospect Elementary
School, Basking Ridge,
New Jersey.
Teacher: Susan Bivona

# You're Quite a Character!

## Objectives

Students are read to or read stories with strong characterization and identify specific character traits with descriptive adjectives.

Students sculpt puppet characters emphasizing mood and personality through facial expressions and body language.

Students convert stories into narrative scripts for puppet performances.

Students perform before a live audience using clear, understandable speech.

## Multiple Intelligences

| Bodily-kinesthetic | Linguistic |
|---|---|
| Interpersonal | |

## National Standards

| | |
|---|---|
| **Visual Arts Standard #2** Using knowledge of structures and functions **Visual Arts Standard #6** Making connections between visual arts and other disciplines | *Grades K-6* **English Language Arts Standard #2** Students read a wide range of literature from many periods in many genres to build an understanding of the many dimensions (e.g., philosophical, ethical, aesthetic) of human experience. **English Language Arts Standard #5** Students employ a wide range of strategies as they write and use different writing process elements appropriately to communicate with different audiences for a variety of purposes. *Grades 3-6* **English Language Arts Standard #9** Students develop an understanding of and respect for diversity in language use, patterns, and dialects across cultures, ethnic groups, geographic regions, and social roles. **English Language Arts Standard #11** Students participate as knowledgeable, reflective, creative, and critical members of a variety of literacy communities. **English Language Arts Standard #12** Students use spoken, written, and visual language to accomplish their own purposes (e.g., for learning, enjoyment, persuasion, and the exchange of information). |

## Background Information

Storytelling is a very old way of sharing information from generation to generation. Puppets are often used to help tell stories. Shadow, rod, and marionette puppets were and still are used in ancient China and other parts of Asia. In Japan, rod puppetry is used as a way of conveying very complex moods and emotions to audiences.

Both storytelling and the use of puppets are considered by many as a natural way for children to express themselves creatively and convey ideas.

## Resources

*A Ring of Tricksters: Animal Tales From America, the West Indies, and Africa* by Virginia Hamilton
Older elementary students readily identify human traits of 11 animal tricksters of African origin. The use of vernacular introduces dialect and cultural variants. Vivid illustrations and a wide variety of opportunities for character study.

*Puppet Mania: The World's Most Incredible Puppet Making Book Ever* by Robert E. Kennedy
Study in characterization as well as puppet design by a former member of Jim Henson's Company. Provides excellent tips for elementary school puppeteers. Directions for 13 projects and ideas for creative expansion.

*Sister Tricksters: Rollicking Tales of Clever Females* by Robert D. San Souci
Collection of eight trickster tales by an award-winning author. Introduces third through sixth graders to eight strong female characters. Richly detailed illustrations provide inspiration for puppet making.

*The Rain Came Down* by David Shannon
A laugh-out-loud story of grumpy neighbors plagued by a rainy day. Provides K to 2 students with a wide assortment of vividly portrayed characters for puppet making.

## Vocabulary List

*Use this list to explore new vocabulary, create idea webs, or brainstorm related subjects. Select words most appropriate to students' ages and abilities.*

- Characterization

| | | |
|---|---|---|
| Adjectives | Generous | Sly |
| Character traits | Intelligent | Smart |
| Clever | Jealous | Stalwart |
| Courageous | Kind | Strong |
| Ferocious | Lively | Sociable |
| Flirtatious | Selfish | Trickster |
| Friendly | Shy | Vivacious |

- Puppetry

| | | |
|---|---|---|
| Bunraku theater | Form | Shadow puppets |
| Design | Hand puppets | Texture |
| Dimension | Lengthwise | Theater |
| Drama | Marionettes | Variety |
| Facial features | Proportion | |
| Finger puppets | Rod puppets | |

Artwork by students
from St. Theresa School,
Hellertown, Pennsylvania.

Dragon 1: You
think you can
defeat me?

Artwork by students from
Mt. Prospect Elementary School,
Basking Ridge, New Jersey.
Teacher: Nancy Knutsen

## What Does It Mean?

**Armature:** a skeletal framework or support on
which a figure is constructed in clay, wax, plaster,
or other media

**Bunraku:** a form of Japanese puppet theater in which
puppeteers, dressed in black and visible to the audience,
manipulate large puppets to the accompaniment of a
chanted narration or musical instrument

**Narrative:** representing stories or events pictorially
or sculpturally

Artwork by students from
CS 102, Bronx, New York.
Teacher: Neila P. Steiner

Crayola

Dream~Makers®
Building fun and creativity into standards-based learning

| | K-2 | 3-4 | 5-6 |
|---|---|---|---|
| Suggested Preparation and Discussion | Tell children they will make puppet figures of their characters. Discuss how a puppet's appearance can convey character. What does a shy person look like? How would a showoff dress? How do you know if someone is friendly? Display a variety of character puppets including examples of the type students will make. Share several fiction or non-fiction books that describe interesting characters. Discuss similarities and differences about book characters using descriptive language. | | |
| Crayola® Supplies | • Construction Paper™ Crayons    • Glitter Glue    • Gel Markers    • Model Magic®    • School Glue    • Scissors | | |
| Other Materials | | • Brown lunch bags    • Construction paper<br>• Craft materials such as feathers, craft eyes, or sequins (optional)<br>• Modeling tools    • Recycled brown grocery bags    • Wooden toothpicks | |
| | • Tablet paper | | |
| Set-up/Tips | | • Use crumpled foil or newspaper as a head armature onto which Model Magic compound is applied.<br>• Embed toothpicks into facial features that need support, such as horns, crowns, or ears. Use caution when working with toothpicks as the wood can be rough and may contain splinters.<br>• Applying marker to moist Model Magic compound results in a soft, watercolor wash effect. | |

**Indonesian Carved Wooden Stick Puppet**
Circa 1980s
Artist unknown
Wood, paint, batik fabric, felt, sequins and string
27" x 7" x 3"
Indonesia
Private Collection.

**Japanese Porcelain Doll**
Circa 18th century
Artist unknown
Porcelain, glass, wood, silk fabric
Kyoto, Japan
Private Collection.

| | K-2 | 3-4 | 5-6 |
|---|---|---|---|
| **Process Session 1 10-20 min.** | **Identify a character** 1. Discuss characters that were presented in literature. How might they look when portrayed in a puppet? Choose one character to represent in a finger puppet. | **Identify character and features** 1. Discuss and select a character from literature. 2. List descriptive words about the character's features and personality. | **Identify character and features** 1. Do advanced research about a character from literature. Pay particular attention to the detail of the characters features. 2. List synonymous words aligned to the character. |
| **Process: Session 2 30-45 min.** | **Make finger puppets** 2. Roll small Model Magic spheres. Push sphere on a finger. Model a body or base on which to create the finger puppet. 3. Add simple three-dimensional forms such as spheres, cubes, cylinders, pyramids, and coils to represent the features of the character. Air-dry puppets for 24 hours. | **Sculpt puppet heads and handles** 3. Roll construction paper from the shorter side into a tight tube. Glue. Press edge until it is secure. Air-dry the glue. 4. Form Model Magic puppet head. Knead color from a marker into white modeling compound to get desired colors. Shape head around the handle. 5. Add ears, nose, and other facial features in appropriate proportions to convey the features and personality of the character. Use modeling tools so puppet has detailed features of the character. Insert feathers and other decorative objects if desired. Air-dry puppets for at least 24 hours. | |
| **Process: Session 3 20-30 min.** | 4. Adults capture ideas on paper for younger students and write a script. Write dialogue for each puppet. | **Finish puppets** 6. Decorate the handle and head with marker and glitter glue. 7. Decorate a paper lunch bag for the character's costume. Cut out and glue paper shapes to the bag for, legs, arms, hands, and feet. | |
| **Process: Session 4 20-30 min.** | **Perform script** 5. A student narrator reads the scripts as others act out their characters' roles. | **Write and perform a play script** 8. Form teams of three students. Brainstorm script ideas using the puppets created by team members. 9. Write dialogue for each puppet represented. 10. Attach scripts to backs of puppets. 11. Read from the scripts. Take turns performing skits for each other. | |
| **Assessment** | • Are the appropriate characters represented to tell a story? Are simple geometric forms identifiable in the finger puppet? • Can viewers identify the character portrayed by each puppet? | • Is puppet workable? Does structure lend itself to function? Does the puppet match the descriptive adjectives? • Does the written material on the back of the puppet include interactive dialogue? • Did students work cooperatively to present an entertaining, cohesive puppet show? | |
| | • Ask students to reflect on this lesson and write a DREAM statement to summarize the most important things they learned. | | |
| **Extensions** | Encourage children to use puppets to narrate segments of the stories they read. Challenge exceptional students to imagine an alternate ending to their play and act with a narrator. Perform skits for an audience of older students, families, school staff, and others in the community. | Perform skits for an audience of younger children. Fasten cue cards to the back of the theater. Establish an artist-in-residence program. Invite a professional puppeteer to share techniques with students. Encourage gifted writers to create original play scripts complete with characters, actions, and settings. Recruit a local author to share strategies for character development. | |

Crayola Dream~Makers®
Building fun and creativity into standards-based learning

# Biographical Treasures

## Objectives

Students are read to or read biographical stories about Asian cultures.

Students interview friends or family to gather information with which to write biographical or autobiographical paragraphs that reflect family anecdotes.

Students (grades 5-6) write autobiographies on the back of a paper kimono model.

Students (grades K-4) design and construct a sagemono or inro, with netske and ojimi beads.

## Multiple Intelligences

Interpersonal

Intrapersonal

Linguistic

## What Does It Mean?

**Anecdote:** short account of an event of an interesting or amusing nature, often biographical

**Character sketch:** short description of a person

**Vessel:** a container, usually for holding liquids

## National Standards

| Visual Arts Standard #4 | English Language Arts Standard #1 |
|---|---|
| Understanding the visual arts in relation to history and cultures | Students read a wide range of print and nonprint texts to build an understanding of texts, of themselves, and of the cultures of the United States and the world; to acquire new information; to respond to the needs and demands of society and the workplace; and for personal fulfillment. Among these texts are fiction and nonfiction, classic and contemporary works. |
| | **English Language Arts Standard #4** |
| | Students adjust their use of spoken, written, and visual language to accomplish their own purposes (e.g., conventions, style, vocabulary) to communicate effectively with a variety of audiences and for different purposes. |

## Background Information

Japanese kimonos traditionally had no pockets. People who wore kimonos carried their money and personal belongings in a small pouch called a sagemono (pronounced sah geh mo no) or inro (pronounced ee n ro). The sagemono was suspended by a cord from the obi (sash) of the kimono. At the top of the cord was a netsuke (pronounced neh ts keh), which looped over the obi to keep the sagemono in place.

Netsuke beads were sometimes carved from ivory and were used to close and lock the sagemono, helping to keep contents inside the sagemono. Smaller beads called ojimo (pronounced o gee meh) were slid up and down a cord connecting the netsuke to the sagemono to regulate the opening and closing of the sagemono. Netsuke and ojimo beads are often created to reflect animals and things from nature.

Biographies and autobiographies are an important form of literature. Both forms of writing often include anecdotes. An anecdote is a short, written piece that tells the story of one incident in a person's life. Anecdotes are often humorous. They are the "remember when" type of stories that are often told and retold at family gatherings.

Artwork by students from Mt. Prospect Elementary School, Basking Ridge, New Jersey.
Teacher: Susan Bivona

## Resources

*Grandfather's Journey* by Allen Say
Recounts the emigration of the author's grandfather from Japan to the United States. Picture book won the 1994 Caldecott Award for illustrations. Evocative of a family album.

*Hands on Asia: Art Activities for All Ages* by Yvonne Y. Merrill
Rich resource of cultural information. Clear folk craft instructions for every age. Illustrated with line drawings and brilliant photographs.

*Red Scarf Girl* by Ji Li Jiang
Autobiography of a 12-year-old Chinese girl caught up in the throes of the Cultural Revolution in 1966. Gives older elementary students insight into the life of a child in another culture.

*Sadako and the Thousand Paper Cranes* by Eleanor Coerr
Inspiring true story of a Japanese girl affected by the bombing of Hiroshima. An excellent introduction to biographical writing for ages 8 to 10.

## Vocabulary List

*Use this list to explore new vocabulary, create idea webs, or brainstorm related subjects.*

| | |
|---|---|
| Anecdote | Nonfiction |
| Authentic | Obi |
| Autobiography | Ojime |
| Bead | Passport |
| Biography | Replica |
| Birthplace | Sagemono |
| Character sketch | Self-portrait |
| Culture | Texture |
| Incident | Toggle |
| Japanese | Tradition |
| Kimono | Vessel |
| Narrative | |
| Netsuke | |

Artwork by students from
Mountainside Elementary School,
Fort Carson, Colorado.
Teacher: Ramona Lapsley

Artwork by students from
St. Theresa School,
Hellertown, Pennsylvania.

# Biographical Treasures

| | K-2 | 3-4 | 5-6 |
|---|---|---|---|
| **Suggested Preparation and Discussion** | Post photographs and pictures that illustrate a Japanese kimono, inro, and a sagemono. Show reproductions of examples of netsuke and ojime beads. Discuss these objects. <br><br> What is a biography? What is an autobiography? Read at least one biographical story, either together or independently. Integrate the material with social studies or history content when possible. <br><br> Display biographies and autobiographies as well as books about Japanese culture. <br><br> Discuss and talk about anecdotes and how they are important to biographical or autobiographical literature. | | |
| **Crayola® Supplies** | • Colored Pencils   • Gel Markers   • Paint Brushes   • Scissors   • School Glue   • Watercolors | | |
| | • Model Magic® | | |
| **Other Materials** | • Index cards   • Recycled newspaper   • Ribbon, yarn, or jute   • Water containers   • White paper | | |
| | • Brown paper lunch bags   • Construction paper (dark colors) <br> • Corrugated cardboard   • Hole punch <br> • Modeling tools such as plastic dinnerware, wooden toothpicks, and craft sticks   • Plastic drinking straws | | • Brown craft paper |
| **Set-up/Tips** | • Cover painting surface with newspaper. | | |
| **Process Session 1 20-30 min.** | **Research biographies and autobiographies** <br> 1. Talk about and discuss the term biography and autobiography. Discuss the similarities and differences. Students interview friends or family about the memories they have of the students. <br> 2. Ask students to make a series of index cards titled "Things that happened to me!" that list events in at least one day in their lives. Younger students may need assistance with writing. Older students include anecdotes. | | |
| | 3. Decorate the borders of the index cards. Arrange in sequence. Punch holes in the top corners. Tie with ribbon. | 3. Interview friends or family about one person. | 3. Conduct autobiographical research through interviews with family and friends. Take notes. |
| **Process: Session 2 30-45 min.** | **Prepare autobiography** <br> 4. Fold paper to form a booklet. Using cards and interview information, write an autobiographical paragraph. <br> 5. Add a title and illustrate the cover. Decorate booklet with patterns and designs. | **Write a biographical sketch** <br> 4. Fold paper to form a booklet. Write a biographical paragraph about the person. <br> 5. Add a title and illustrate the front cover. Decorate booklet with patterns and designs. | **Decorate kimono** <br> 4. Students fold brown craft paper in half to equal one half of their bodies. <br> 5. Draw a kimono on the face of the folded paper. <br> 6. Paint authentic Asian shapes and patterns on one side of the kimono. Air-dry the painting. |
| **Process: Session 3 30-45 min.** | **Create a sagemono with netsuke and ojime beads** <br> 6. Form two Ping-Pong ball-sized amounts of Model Magic compound around a straw to create two beads. Cut away excess straw. <br> 7. Use fingers and/or modeling tools to add texture to the beads. The netsuke usually was a character such as a face, mask, animal, or object. Choose something important to the person in the writing. The ojime, for sliding on a cord, was often plain. Air-dry beads for 24 hours. | | **Write an autobiographical sketch** <br> 7. Draw a large rectangle on the back of the kimono. Write the autobiography in this space. |

This photograph illustrates the actual size of a typical netske bead. Ojime beads were similar in size.

| | K-2 | 3-4 | 5-6 |
|---|---|---|---|
| **Process: Session 4** 20-30 min. | **Decorate beads** 8. Paint the beads to enrich them with color. 9. Cover beads with a glaze made from equal parts glue and water. Air-dry the glaze. | | |
| **Process: Session 5** 30-45 min. | **Make sagemono bag** 10. Fill the front and back of a brown paper lunch bag with shapes, patterns, and colors using Gel markers. 11. Cut a 24" cord and fold in half. Thread it through the netsuke bead. Tie ends so bead is locked into position at one end of the cord. 12. Thread remaining cord through ojime bead so it can slide freely along the length of the cord. 13. Cut two strips of 1- x 4 1/2-inch corrugated cardboard. Glue one end of cord under a cardboard piece on each side of the sagemono bag. 14. Put biographical material into sagemono bag. Close and seal with ojime bead. Students who wish may attach netsuke bead to the top of their belts, so the sagemono bag hangs at their sides. | | |

| Assessment |
|---|
| • Do the biographical or autobiographical facts accurately reflect the lives of the writers or their families? • Are projects constructed according to directions? Are they aesthetically pleasing and functional? • Ask students to reflect on this lesson and write a DREAM statement to summarize the most important things they learned. |

| | | |
|---|---|---|
| • Do the index cards record a correct sequence of events? | • Is the biography written in good paragraph form? Is it rich in details? | • Does the autobiographical sketch tell a story with a clear beginning, middle, and end? Does it demonstrate good writing conventions? |

| Extensions |
|---|
| Provide a computer or a scribe for students whose special needs make writing difficult or for emerging writers. |

| | | |
|---|---|---|
| Invite students to tell their stories to others. Where were they born? How were their names chosen? Be aware that some children may not be comfortable discussing this personal information. Encourage students who are gifted writers to write about themselves or about a recent event in their lives. | Interview an interesting member of the school community. Write an article for the school paper. Read biographies about inventors, peacemakers, and other leaders. List questions to ask the person. Reenact what a dinner conversation might be like with these historic figures as guests. | Interview relatives to learn more interesting family anecdotes. Make an illustrated scrapbook of memories and give it as a gift to a family member. Hold a storytelling festival with interesting family anecdotes. |

| | | |
|---|---|---|
| Encourage advanced students to research and share with the class the history of Japanese kimonos, netsuke, ojime, and sagemono. | | Research and design kimonos for various occasions. |

**Old Turtle Netsuke**
Circa 18th century
Artist unknown
Carved ivory
Kyoto, Japan
Private Collection.

Crayola Dream~Makers®
Building fun and creativity into standards-based learning

# Picture-Story Scrolls

## Objectives

Students demonstrate their understanding of the relationship between art and text by creating a narrative picture scroll based on literature.

Students demonstrate their understanding of the story's plot development by breaking it into individual scenes and retelling it through a sequence of visual images and symbols.

Students in grades 3 to 6 embellish their images with text.

Students in grades 5 to 6 prepare a decorated storage box for their scrolls.

## Multiple Intelligences

Linguistic
Logical-mathematical
Spatial

## What Does It Mean?

**Pictograph:** artwork that shows people, places, and/or things in pictures, signs, or symbols

**Narrative picture scroll:** story told through illustration without text on a single, long surface

## National Standards

| Visual Arts Standard #6<br>Making connections between visual arts and other disciplines | English Language Arts Standard #7<br>Students conduct research on issues and interests by generating ideas and questions, and by posing problems. They gather, evaluate and synthesize data from a variety of sources (e.g., print and non-print texts, artifacts, people) to communicate their discoveries in ways that suit their purpose and audience.<br><br>English Language Arts Standard #12<br>Students use spoken, written and visual language to accomplish their own purposes (e.g., for learning, enjoyment, persuasion, and the exchange of information). |
| --- | --- |

## Background Information

A Japanese masterpiece, the narrative picture scroll Ban Dainagon Ekotoba (Story of the Courtier Ban Dainagon), tells the historical tale of a complicated power struggle among the Japanese aristocracy in the early Heian Period (9th century). A nobleman scheming for promotion at court deliberately set fire to a gate of the Imperial Palace and accused a high government official of arson. The truth was discovered when a child who witnessed the crime revealed the true culprit. As a result, the scheming nobleman was exiled.

This scroll is one of the most precious works of its type, representing the zenith of the art of Japanese narrative picture scrolls. Scholars believe it was produced in the late Heian Period (12th century), about 300 years after the historical event it depicts.

The story of the Courtier Ban Dainagon also exists in written form in the Uji Shui Monogatari (Tales Collected by the Courtier Uji), one of the great literary works of the Kamakura Period (13th century).

## Resources

*Anno's Journey* by Mitsumasa Anno
A visual journey through time and place in which viewers encounter delightful visual surprises, from familiar storybook characters to scenes from famous paintings. All ages will be intrigued.

*Flotsam* by David Wiesner
In this fascinating fantasy, a boy discovers a camera and develops the film. He records his own role in this series of events and tosses the camera back into the ocean. An intricately detailed story told entirely through pictures. Geared to grades K to 4, but will be appreciated by all ages.

*How and Why Stories* by Martha Hamilton
Winner of the 2000 Parents' Choice Award, this collection of short stories from around the world is an excellent resource for older elementary students. Plot lines are simple and direct and can easily be retold in picture format.

*The Snowman* by Raymond Briggs
A warm story of friendship between a snowman and a young boy that reminds readers of how fleeting life can be. This wordless picture book with a message for everyone is also available as a short film.

## Vocabulary List

*Use this list to explore new vocabulary, create idea webs, or brainstorm related subjects.*

Characters
Chronological
Fairy tale
Flotsam
Folk tale
Linear perspective
Narrative
Pictographs
Picture-story
Plot
Scenes
Scroll
Sequence
Series
Setting
Storyboard
Tiered perspective

Artwork by students from
Rockway Elementary School,
Rockway, Florida.
Teacher: Kathleen Hull

Artwork by students from
Tanglewood Elementary School,
Fort Worth, Texas.
Teacher: Jessica Patterson

Artwork by students from
Mt. Prospect Elementary School,
Basking Ridge, New Jersey.
Teachers: Regina DeFrancisco,
Susan Bivona

Crayola

Dream~Makers®
Building fun and creativity into standards-based learning

# Picture-Story Scrolls

| | K-2 | 3-4 | 5-6 |
|---|---|---|---|
| **Suggested Preparation and Discussion** | Display and review a variety of wordless picture books as well as an example of the Japanese scroll project. Share background information about Japanese story scrolls. ||
| | Select one book and discuss the content. Pose questions such as, What do the pictures reveal about characters and settings? What is the story problem? Identify several key events. How is the problem resolved? |||
| | Discuss how to transfer the sequence of text into the sequence of visual imagery. For example, ask students to visualize and discuss how they might retell the story using only pictures. Think in terms of scenes or events rather than words. |||
| | Assemble a library of classic fairy tales with simple plot lines such as *The Three Little Pigs*. Ask students to visualize story details. | Collect and make available American folk tales such as the Jack tales, Uncle Remus stories, or tall tale heroes such as Paul Bunyan and Pecos Bill for students to read. | Gather a collection of fiction and non-fiction literature. Discuss details of the stories and how students can transfer text to imagery. |
| | Make an example of a picture story scroll to show students. |||
| **Crayola® Supplies** | • Colored Pencils  • Paint Brushes  • School Glue  • Scissors  • Tempera Paint  • Watercolors |||
| **Other Materials** | • Brown paper grocery bags  • Cardboard  • Paper plates  • Paper towels  • Recycled newspaper <br> • Ribbon, yarn, or cord  • Rubber bands  • Rulers  • Water containers  • White drawing paper  • White paper |||
| | | | • Shoeboxes |
| **Set-up/Tips** | • Cover painting surface with recycled newspaper. Use paper plates as palettes for students to share. <br> • Apply small amounts of glue and lots of pressure to speed the drying process. <br> • Ask families to provide clean, recycled shoe boxes. |||
| **Process: Session 1 30-45 min.** | **Make a scroll** <br> 1. Cut brown paper grocery bags into two 6- x 24-inch rectangles. <br> 2. Roll each rectangle to create a tight 6-inch long cylinder. Glue edges securely. Wrap with rubber bands to air-dry glue. Remove rubber bands when dry. <br> 3. Fold two or three sheets of drawing paper in half. Cut along the folds. Glue the pieces together end to end to create one, long continuous paper. Glue one cylinder to each of the ends. Hold in place until air-dry. |||

**Ban Dainagon Ekotoba (Story of the Courtier Ban Dainagon)**
Reproduction based on narrative picture scroll
and hardwood container, color on paper.
Vol. 1, 31.5 X 825.3 cm
Heian Period, silk, paper, wood, ivory.
12th century.
Designated National Treasure by
Japanese Government.
Private Collection.

| | K-2 | 3-4 | 5-6 |
|---|---|---|---|
| **Process:** Session 2 30-45 min. | **Decorate scroll backing** 4. Spread out scroll, back side up. Squeeze gold tempera on paper plates. Spread paint on plate with a cardboard scrap. Crumple a piece of paper towel, dab it in the paint, then dab it randomly over the back of the scroll to create a textured effect. Leave some areas unpainted. Repeat with other colors. Air-dry flat. | | |
| **Process:** Session 3 20-30 min. | **Prepare background wash** 5. With scroll face up, brush clean water over the surface. Moisten watercolor cakes. Apply a watercolor wash horizontally along the moist scroll until desired background effect is achieved. Air-dry flat. | | |
| **Process:** Session 4 30-45 min. or more | **Plan horizontal narrative pictures** 6. Select at least three major scenes from stories to illustrate on a horizontally positioned scroll. 7. Sketch plans to depict the main character and the setting. Show the problem, key events, and the outcome. Create a sense of action to coincide with the plot line. | **Plan vertical narrative pictures** 6. Select at least five major scenes from stories to illustrate on a vertically positioned scroll. 7. Sketch scenes to depict the main character and the setting. Show the problem, several key events, and the outcome. Create a sense of action to coincide with the plot line. Identify captions or speech balloons to embellish the story. | |
| **Process:** Session 5 30-45 min. | **Illustrate the scroll** 8. On the scroll, draw and color scenes in the story sequence with colored pencils. 9. Show details to clearly convey setting, action, and outcome. | **Complete illustrations and text** 8. On the scroll, use the plan to draw and color scenes in the story sequence with colored pencils. 9. Write simple text that is correlated to the images. Use words to clarify points and enhance characterizations. | |
| | 10. Roll both ends of the cylinders toward the center. Tie closed with ribbon. | | |
| **Process:** Session 6 30-45 min. | | | **Create scroll storage container** 11. Wrap a shoebox and its lid separately in paper. Glue in place. 12. Design a block letter title correlated to the scroll story on the lid. Embellish the title and surrounding area with watercolor. Air-dry the paint. 13. Decorate the box with scenes that reflect the story on the scroll. |

**Assessment**

- Do images on the scroll accurately correlate to the text in the readings? Is the story problem clearly pictured and are key events arranged in a logical sequence? Is there a satisfying conclusion to the story through images and/or text?
- Is the scroll sturdily made according to directions and easy to handle? Does the project show evidence of control over the medium and age-appropriate skill in the use of artistic techniques?
- Ask students to reflect on this lesson and write a DREAM statement to summarize the most important things they learned.

**Extensions**

Young children and children with special needs may have better success if they work in groups, with each child creating one illustration on separate paper. When all are finished, students work together to arrange the pictures in a logical sequence. Glue pictures together end to end and attach the cylinders.

Invite older students or those with advanced skills to create films based on their story scrolls. Suggest that they view the film version of Raymond Brigg's wordless picture book, *The Snowman*, for filmmaking ideas.

Invite a professional storyteller to present a performance and talk with students about story imaging.

Hold a storytelling festival. Students show their scrolls and tell the accompanying story.

# Define & Design a Dictionary

## Objectives

Students learn new vocabulary words found in works of fiction and nonfiction literature.

Students use dictionaries and other resources to correlate words with definitions and synonyms.

Students construct a three-dimensional tower to be used as a repository to store newly learned vocabulary words and their meanings.

## Multiple Intelligences

Intrapersonal
Linguistic

## What Does It Mean?

**Etymology:** study of historical linguistic change, especially individual words

**Three-dimensional tower:** a tall structure made with various materials

## National Standards

| **Visual Arts Standard #2** Using knowledge of structures and functions | **English Language Arts Standard #3** Students apply a wide range of strategies to comprehend, interpret, evaluate, and appreciate texts. They draw on their prior experience, their interactions with other readers and writers, their knowledge of word meaning and of other texts, their word identification strategies, and their understanding of textual features (e.g., sound-letter correspondence, sentence structure, context, graphics). |
| --- | --- |

## Background Information

The creation of the *Oxford English Dictionary (OED)* began in 1857. It took 70 years to complete. The dictionary contains 414,825 definitions. Behind the making of the dictionary are two amazing men.

Professor James Murray was the editor of the OED project. Dr. William Chester Minor, a Civil War surgeon originally from New Haven, Connecticut, helped write the dictionary. Minor was no ordinary contributor. He sent thousands of handwritten quotations from his home in the small village of Crowthorne, 50 miles from Oxford, to Professor Murray to help write the book.

The two men corresponded with each other often during the writing of the dictionary. In 1896, after Minor had sent nearly 10,000 definitions to the dictionary, Murray and Minor finally met each other.

## Resources

*Donovan's Word Jar* by MonaLisa DeGross and Cheryl Hanna
A third-grade boy is so fascinated by words that he collects them on slips of paper and keeps them in a glass jar. This book will introduce young students to the delight of new and interesting words.

*Hailstones and Halibut Bones* by Mary O'Neill
The value of using specific details and vocabulary to enhance writing is exemplified for older elementary and middle school students in this collection of poems about colors. "Red is a lipstick, Red is a shout, Red is a signal that says: Watch out!'" (unpaged)

*Her Stories—African American Folktales, Fairy Tales and True Tales told* by Virginia Hamilton
Rich anthology of stories inspires older students looking for ways to use words to express thoughts, feelings, and personal experiences.

*The Alphabet Tree* by Leo Lionni
Picture book introduces the concept that words can be put together to make meaning.

*The Place My Words Are Looking For: What Poets Say About and Through Their Work* by Paul B. Janeczko
Anthology for older elementary children. Includes commentary by 39 poets about how and why they love and use words. Gwendolyn Brooks tells readers to "COLLECT WORDS!... CIRCLE exciting words. The more words you know, the better you will be able to express yourself." (p. 62)

## Vocabulary List

*As students study words, they may come across terms such as these. Focus on those that are appropriate for the age and ability levels of the children in your class.*

- Language arts vocabulary

| | | |
| --- | --- | --- |
| Antonym | Denotation | Symmetry |
| Balance | Dictionary | Synonym |
| Connotation | Etymology | Thesaurus |
| Definition | Origin | |

- Parts of speech vocabulary

| | | |
| --- | --- | --- |
| Adjective | Interjection | Pronoun |
| Adverb | Noun | Verb |
| Conjunction | Preposition | |

Artwork by students from
Mt. Prospect Elementary School,
Basking Ridge, New Jersey.
Teacher: Rebecca Murphy

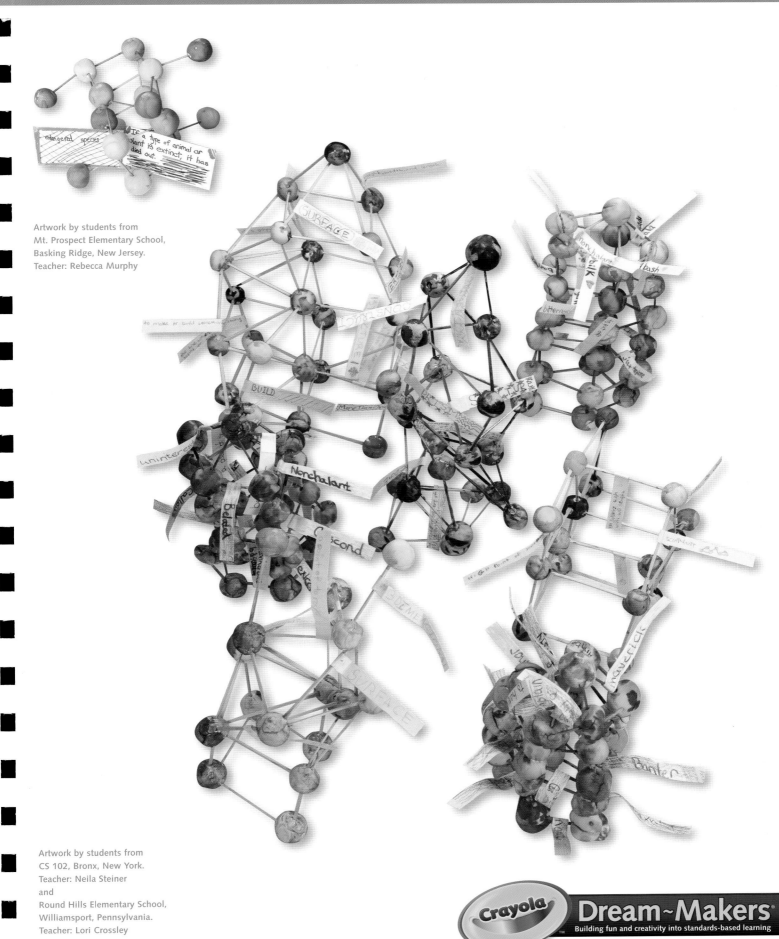

Artwork by students from
Mt. Prospect Elementary School,
Basking Ridge, New Jersey.
Teacher: Rebecca Murphy

Artwork by students from
CS 102, Bronx, New York.
Teacher: Neila Steiner
and
Round Hills Elementary School,
Williamsport, Pennsylvania.
Teacher: Lori Crossley

# Define & Design a Dictionary

| | K-2 | 3-4 | 5-6 |
|---|---|---|---|
| **Suggested Preparation and Discussion** | Explain that each student will make a word tower using some new words and their definitions. Encourage older students to use a thesaurus as a source for selecting words for their towers. Assemble a resource center in the classroom that includes dictionaries and thesauruses. Select age-appropriate vocabulary words aligned to literature readings. Students write them on index cards. Create and display a model dictionary tower that includes sample words and definitions. Talk about how to construct a tower. | | |
| **Crayola® Supplies** | • Colored Pencils • Model Magic® (white) • Paint Brushes • School Glue • Scissors • Watercolors | | |
| **Other Materials** | • Masking tape • Paper towels • Recycled newspaper • Recycled shoeboxes • Rulers • Water containers • White drawing paper • Wooden toothpicks | | |
| **Set-up/Tips** | • Use shoeboxes or similar containers to store pieces between sessions. Ask families to donate clean, recycled boxes. <br> • Cover the painting area with newspaper. <br> • It is imperative to air-dry the Model Magic spheres for 24 hours before assembling them into a structure. Dried spheres provide significant support as the tower grows taller. Younger students or those with motor disabilities could construct a cube or pyramid to simplify stability issues. | | |
| **Process: Session 1 30-45 min. or more** | **Identify words** <br> 1. Students list words they have recently learned in their reading. <br> 2. As a group, talk about what they mean. Where can they find definitions of words they don't know? <br> 3. Discuss what a group of words that expresses a thought or idea is called. Choose at least six new words to portray on a word tower. | **Identify words and definitions** <br> 1. Students share at least six new and interesting vocabulary words they learned recently in their assigned readings. <br> 2. Elicit definitions. Look up puzzling words in dictionaries to compare definitions. <br> 3. Choose at least six words from the list to portray on a word tower. | **Identify words and synonyms** <br> 1. Encourage students to think of ways to vary vocabulary in their writing. Start by identifying at least eight common words such as *said*, *went*, and *put*. Post them for all to see. <br> 2. Students suggest alternatives to these words. A student recorder adds the alternatives to the list. Look up words in a thesaurus and list more possibilities. Look up these synonyms in dictionaries and share definitions. Talk about fine lines of meaning. Is there a difference, for example, between *ambled* and *strode*? <br> 3. Students list as many synonyms as they can (at least eight) for various hues of a color—or any other vocabulary related to current language arts studies. |
| **Process: Session 2 5-10 min.** | **Construct tower spheres** <br> 4. Students roll six (or more for grades 5-6) Ping-Pong ball sized Model Magic spheres. Air-dry for 24 hours. | | |
| **Process: Session 3 20-30 min.** | **Paint tower spheres** <br> 5. Paint the spheres with watercolors. Use multiple coats for more intense hues. Air-dry the paint. | | |

| | K-2 | 3-4 | 5-6 |
|---|---|---|---|
| **Process: Session 4** 15-20 min. | **Write words and symbols** 6. Cut six 2" x 10" paper rectangles. 7. Print one new word on each rectangle, leaving a 1/2" margin on the left edge. Refer to the list to spell the words correctly. 8. Draw a symbol correlated to the word on the reverse side of each rectangle. | **Write words and definitions** 6. Cut a 2" x 10" paper rectangle for each word chosen. 7. Write one vocabulary word on side of the rectangle and the definition on the other side. 8. Add decorative shapes and patterns surrounding the words and definitions. | **Write words and synonyms** 6. Cut at least eight 2" x 10" paper rectangles. 7. Write a vocabulary word on half of the rectangle and a synonym on the other half of the same side. 8. Add decorative shapes and patterns surrounding the synonyms. |

| **Process: Session 5** 30-45 min. | **Construct towers** 9. Insert toothpicks into one sphere to begin a square. Create a second square shape from spheres and toothpicks. 10. Join the two squares with additional toothpicks to create a sturdy cube. Use this cube as the foundation on which to build the tower. Glue toothpicks in place. Air-dry the glue. |
|---|---|

| **Process: Session 6** 10-15 min. | **Add words** 11. Glue word strips to toothpicks on the tower. Air-dry the glue before handling. |
|---|---|

| **Assessment** | • Has the student's attention to balance and symmetry created a stable tower? Does the use of color create an attractive overall effect? • Are words clearly written, correctly spelled, and accurately defined or (grades 5-6) matched with synonyms? Do symbols correlate to word strips created by younger students? • Ask students to reflect on this lesson and write a DREAM statement to summarize the most important things they learned. |
|---|---|

| **Extensions** | Encourage younger students and those with some types of learning disabilities to select concrete words that can be represented with symbols. Students take turns reading aloud the words on their towers. Consider using them to play a game of charades. Use the words in round-robin creative sentences, poetry, or storytelling. | Write short stories or poems inspired by the words on the towers. Illustrate them in appealing formats such as triaramas or comic strips. Ask reporters, authors, public speakers, editors, librarians, and others who deal with words daily to read books aloud with the class. What techniques do they use to make the words come alive? Hold a "definition bee" similar to a spelling bee. For even more fun, invite children's families to be part of the experience. | Write descriptive paragraphs or poems using words from the towers. Gifted students work in small groups to write and perform one-act plays using their words and alternatives. |
|---|---|---|---|

As students learn additional vocabulary, add more spheres, toothpick bars, and word strips to towers.

Children's Building Blocks
Painted wood
Private Collection.

# Accordion Books for Marvelous Miniature Libraries

## Objectives

Students analyze and discuss their literary reading, focusing on the people, places, and/or things revealed within the context of the stories.

Students make accordion books that include text and images related to their readings.

Students in grades 5 and 6 create storage containers that serve as "miniatures libraries" to hold their books.

Students are read to or read assigned fiction or non-fiction literature.

## Multiple Intelligences

Bodily-kinesthetic
Linguistic
Spatial

## What Does It Mean?

**Accordion-fold book:** book with pleated pages

**Aesthetically pleasing:** artwork that contains features that are satisfying to the mind and emotions, reflecting one's sense of beauty

## National Standards

| | |
|---|---|
| **Visual Arts Standard #2** Using knowledge of structures and functions **Visual Arts Standard #6** Making connections between visual arts and other disciplines | **English Language Arts Standard #3** Students apply a wide range of strategies to comprehend, interpret, evaluate, and appreciate texts. They draw on their prior experience, their interactions with other readers and writers, their knowledge of word meaning and of other texts, their word identification strategies, and their understanding of textual features (e.g., sound-letter correspondence, sentence structure, context, graphics). **English Language Arts Standard #8** Students use a variety of technological and information resources (e.g., libraries, databases, computer networks, video) to gather and synthesize information and to create and communicate knowledge. **English Language Arts Standard #12** Students use spoken, written, and visual language to accomplish their own purposes (e.g., for learning, enjoyment, persuasion, and the exchange of information). |

## Background Information

Mesopotamian clay tablets and ancient Egyptian papyrus scrolls are evidence of a longstanding interest in written records. Aristotle founded the Great Library of Alexandria, Egypt, in 300 BCE. The library was destroyed 1,600 years ago but was recently replaced by a new library that will eventually hold 8 million books.

In the 1400s, Gutenberg's invention of moveable type transformed the book production process, making it possible to print multiple copies quickly without laborious hand copying. Soon, national libraries were established, including the Bibliotheque Nationale de France in 1367 and the British Library in 1759.

The oldest library in the United States began in 1638 with a 400-book donation by John Harvard to a new university that later adopted his name. In 1731 Ben Franklin established the Library Company of Philadelphia. The United States Library of Congress was founded in 1800 with a $5,000 grant from Congress. It was expanded in 1815 with the addition of Thomas Jefferson's vast collection. In 1833 the first public library in the United States opened in Peterborough, New Hampshire.

## Resources

*Hand-Made Books: An Introduction to Bookbinding* by Rob Shepherd
Directions for 10 different projects made from common household materials. Close-up photos of tools and processes. Demonstrates use of decorative and marbled papers for cover designs. All ages.

*Inkheart* by Cornelia Funke
Tale of a suspense-filled story about 12-year-old Meggie, whose father can "read" characters to life. Will intrigue advanced fifth and sixth grade readers.

*M.C. Escher: Book of Boxes—100 Years 1898-1998* from Benedikt Taschen Verlag
Collection of 21 thin cardboard punch-out designs. Includes illustrated folding directions.

*Wild About Books* by Judy Sierra
Animals in a zoo learn to love reading when Molly McGrew arrives in a bookmobile. Told in lively rhyme. Written especially for K-2, but fun for all booklovers.

## Vocabulary List

*Use this list to explore new vocabulary, create idea webs, or brainstorm related subjects.*

Accordion book
Author
Bibliography
Card catalog
Characterization
Dewey Decimal System
Embellishments
Fiction
Flip book
Illustrator
Library

Library of Congress
Mood
Nonfiction
Opinion
Parchment
Pattern
Plot
Pop-up book

Reference
Repetition
Research
Resource
Setting
Spread
Theme
Variety

Folded Glasses Case Book
Artist: Connie Ashley Akers
Glasses case, paper, paint, ribbon, mixed media
2 1/2" x 5"
Collection of Connie Ashley Akers.

Crayola

**Dream~Makers**
Building fun and creativity into standards-based learning

# Accordion Books for Marvelous Miniature Libraries

| | K-2 | 3-4 | 5-6 |
|---|---|---|---|
| **Suggested Preparation and Discussion** | Display examples of various handmade and/or commercially published miniature books. Create a sample accordion book. For grades 5 and 6, include a miniature box repository. Demonstrate how to make accordion folds and books. | | |
| **Crayola® Supplies** | • Markers   • School Glue   • Scissors | | |
| | | • Paint Brushes   • Tempera Paint   • Watercolor Colored Pencils | |
| | | | • Model Magic® |
| **Other Materials** | • Construction paper   • Recycled file folders or oak tag   • Recycled newspaper   • Ribbon or yarn • White drawing paper | | |
| | | • Leaves or other flat shapes   • Paper plates   • Paper towels • Sandpaper   • Water containers | |
| | | | • Recycled boxes with lids • Sponges   • Textured surfaces • White craft paper |
| **Set-up/Tips** | | • Ask families to save clean cardboard boxes such as shoe boxes. • Cover painting surface with newspaper. • Try several techniques with watercolor pencils. Dip tips in water and draw for intense colors. Draw on dry paper and then use a damp brush to spread the color. | |

**Process: Session 1 30-45 min.**

### Read and discuss literature

1. Children read fiction or nonfiction books appropriate to their literacy levels.
2. With children, identify characters, settings, and storylines that are the focus of the literature. Brainstorm key facts that are relevant to understanding the story.

**Process: Session 2 30 min.**

### Create accordion books

3. Cut file folders into two panels for front and back covers. If desired, cover with construction paper. Glue in place.
4. Cut at least two long strips of paper to make accordion-book pages. Fold and join with glue as needed.
5. Glue ends of ribbon or yarn to inside edges of book cover. Glue book pages on top of ribbon, inside the two covers. Air-dry the books.

**Process: Session 3 30-45 min. or more**

### Add text and illustrations

6. Illustrate one side of the long paper on each of the pages. Show characters, settings, and actions that correlate to the readings.
7. Add word text correlated to illustrations.

**Process: Session 4 30-45 min. or more**

### Decorate back of folded paper

8. Decorate the reverse side of the long paper with colorful patterns and shapes.

### Decorate back of folded paper

8. Brush water over one side of the long paper. Place dried, pressed leaves or other flat shapes on the wet paper.
9. With sandpaper, sand watercolor pencils over the leaves to create a stencil effect. Carefully remove leaves.
10. Add decorative designs to the silhouette leaf shapes using watercolor pencils. Air-dry the paper flat.

**Decorative House Container With Folding Book**
Artist: Connie Ashley Akers
Mixed media
5" x 6" x 8"
Collection of Connie Ashley Akers.

| | K-2 | 3-4 | 5-6 |
|---|---|---|---|
| **Process: Session 5** 10-15 min. | | | **Decorate paper** 11. Place damp sponge on a paper plate. Spread tempera on sponge. Dab stamps on sponge. Press stamp on paper. Repeat to create patterns. Make as many sheets as needed to cover boxes. Air-dry the paint. |
| **Process: Session 6** 20-30 min. | | | **Make a miniature library container** 12. Place box in the center of the stamped paper. Cut paper to cover the box. Glue to box. Do the same with box lid. 13. Fold and tie books. Place them inside containers. |

**Assessment**

• Does paper folding demonstrate an understanding of the accordion fold?

• Ask students to explain why they chose certain colors for their cover designs. Is the design aesthetically pleasing? Are colors reflective of the mood of the story? Is the title and author of the story clearly written on the front cover?

• Are illustrations and text clearly correlated to key event in the literature? Do they follow a logical sequence?

| | |
|---|---|
| | • Are decorations on miniature library containers correlated to the books they hold? • Can students articulate why they selected designs that appear on the containers? |

• Ask students to reflect on this lesson and write a DREAM statement to summarize the most important things they learned.

**Extensions**

Ask an art teacher or local expert to teach the craft of paper making to the class. Make paper for these books or greeting cards.

Set up "book buddies." Older children join younger ones for book sharing once or twice a month. Older students select and read age-appropriate stories and create a related craft with their buddies.

Provide assistance in book assembly for younger students and some with special needs.

Invite children with exceptional spatial intelligence to research and demonstrate designs for origami books and boxes.

Academically talented students might enjoy doing further research on the history of books and libraries.

**How to fold an accordion book**

## Objectives

Students identify a sequence of events from a short fiction story and write and illustrate accordion books demonstrating their understanding of that sequence.

Students (K-4) sequence information from a nonfiction reading selection and create diagrams demonstrating their interpretation of the details, such as food chains or the water cycle.

Student (5-6) identify common idiomatic expressions and demonstrate an understanding of the role sequencing plays in humor by creating flip books illustrating those expressions.

## Multiple Intelligences

| Interpersonal | Logical-mathematical |
|---|---|
| Linguistic | Naturalist |

## National Standards

**Visual Arts Standard #5**
Reflecting upon and assessing the characteristics and merits of their work and the work of others

**Visual Arts Standard #6**
Making connections between visual arts and other disciplines

*Grades K-6*
**English Language Arts Standard #3**
Students apply a wide range of strategies to comprehend, interpret, evaluate, and appreciate texts. They draw on their prior experience, their interactions with other readers and writers, their knowledge of word meaning and of other texts, their word identification strategies, and their understanding of textual features (e.g., sound-letter correspondence, sentence structure, context, graphics).

**English Language Arts Standard #6**
Students apply knowledge of language structure, language conventions (e.g., spelling and punctuation), media techniques, figurative language, and genre to create, critique, and discuss print and nonprint texts.

**English Language Arts Standard #12**
Students use spoken, written, and visual language to accomplish their own purposes (e.g., for learning, enjoyment, persuasion, and the exchange of information).

*Grades 3-4*
**English Language Arts Standard #7**
Students conduct research on issues and interests by generating ideas and questions, and by posing problems. They gather, evaluate, and synthesize data from a variety of sources (e.g., print and nonprint texts, artifacts, people) to communicate their discoveries in ways that suit their purpose and audience.

*Grades 5-6*
**English Language Arts Standard #10**
Students whose first language is not English make use of their first language to develop competency in the English language arts and to develop understanding of content across the curriculum.

## Background Information

A sequence is the following of one thing after another in chronological, causal, or logical order. It shows succession or continuity.

Comic book artists use sequence of drawing and text to reveal their stories and ideas. Text is used minimally to identify settings, show sound effects, or to communicate a character's speech and thoughts in word balloons. In Japan, entire novels are written in this form. In the United States, these are known as graphic novels, book-length stories told in images and words, often with complex plots and serious themes.

Disney Animation Studios and Dreamworks are two organizations that use storyboarding and illustration extensively in their film productions. Animation artists design and lay the groundwork in sketches before final work is started in a feature-length animation film.

## Resources

*Jungle Morph* by Fliptomania
Colorful, fast-paced flipbook. Begins with a tiger which changes into a chimp, then an elephant, and eventually a giraffe. Good example for older elementary students.

*The Very Hungry Caterpillar* by Eric Carle
Classic tale of a caterpillar that turns into a butterfly. Integrates several sequences: days of the week, counting, and a life cycle. Enhances sequencing lessons for early elementary students.

*What Are Food Chains and Webs?* by Bobbie Kalman
Informative text for third and fourth grade research projects about food chains and webs.

*www.usingenglish.com/reference/idioms/*
Alphabetical list of thousands of English idiomatic expressions with clear explanations of what they mean.

## Vocabulary List

*Use this list to explore new vocabulary, create idea webs, or brainstorm related subjects.*

- Food chains

| | | | |
|---|---|---|---|
| Carnivore | Herbivore | Omnivore | Producer |
| Consumer | | | |

- Sequence words

| | | | |
|---|---|---|---|
| Alphabetical | Chronological | Order | Series |
| Arrangement | Direction | Pattern | Succession |

- Sequential transition words

| | | | |
|---|---|---|---|
| Finally | First | Later | Next |
| Then | | | |

- Other words

| | | | |
|---|---|---|---|
| Accordion fold | Contrast | Graphic novel | Movement |
| Balance | Flipbook | Idiomatic expression | Storyboard |

## What Does It Mean?

**Ecosystem:** interaction of a community of organisms with their environment

**Flip book:** format designed to reveal animation action when the pages are quickly changed in order

**Idiomatic expressions:** stylistic phrases that have meaning within the context of the culture or language

The Ocean
Food Chain
Killer Whale
Leopard Seal
Shrimp
Fish
Penguin

How Does A Flower Grow?
By Madeline

First I plant my seed.
Next I water and make sure it gets some sun light.
Finally a beautiful flower sprouts.
The End

Crayola Dream~Makers
Building fun and creativity into standards-based learning

| | K-2 | 3-4 | 5-6 |
|---|---|---|---|
| **Suggested Preparation and Discussion** | Display a collection of stories with clearly sequential plots as well as examples of accordion books.<br><br>Read together *The Very Hungry Caterpillar*. What does the word sequence mean? What sequences occur in this story?<br><br>Children read other books independently or at home to identify three sequential events. | Display reference materials about major ecosystems or other similar sequential material in fields such as science or social studies. Provide pictures of many different plants and animals. Play a mix and match game to introduce the idea of food chains.<br><br>Which animals eat only plants? What are they called? Which animals eat only other animals? What are they called? Which animals eat both plants and animals? What are they called?<br><br>Ask for an example of a sequential food chain. What is an ecosystem? Identify ecosystems in your community. Compare and contrast the foods available in different ecosystems.<br><br>Children form small groups and research different ecosystems. They collect data to graphically represent in food web diagrams. | Collect comic strips, jokes, and anecdotes where humor is dependent upon sequential presentation. Share several jokes and anecdotes with class. Discuss verbal humor. What makes something funny?<br><br>Display examples of flipbooks. With students, research and post list of idiomatic expressions.<br><br>Provide small groups of students with cut-up comic strips. Challenge them to reconstruct the jokes by arranging segments in proper sequence.<br><br>Share funny idiomatic expressions. *(I have a frog in my throat.)* What does the expression mean? What might a non-native speaker of English picture? How could this be visually portrayed in a humorous flip book? What picture should come first? second? third? |
| **Crayola® Supplies** | • Colored Pencils  • Crayons<br>• Scissors | • Fine Line Markers | • Crayons<br>• Fine Line Markers (black) |
| | | • Markers | |
| **Other Materials** | | • Tablet paper | • Stapler |
| | • White drawing paper (18 x 24 inches) | | |
| **Process: Session 1**<br><br>**Grades K-4**<br>**20-30 min.**<br><br>**Grades 5-6**<br>**45-60 min.** | **Create accordion books**<br>1. Cut drawing paper into a 6" x 24" strip. Fold strip twice to make a 6-page accordion book. Make the first flap the front cover. Number the pages on the inside.<br>2. Write a sentence at the bottom of each inside page describing one of three sequential events from independent reading. | **Prepare sketch**<br>1. Students share data within their groups and determine examples of sequential food chains for their chosen ecosystems.<br>2. Plan layout for poster design. Include space for a title, a large bull's-eye diagram with arrows, and pictures of specific plants and animals, as well as labels and simple text. Consider size and balance of design. | **Prepare flipbooks**<br>1. Students cut white drawing paper into 10 to 15 small pages uniform in size.<br>2. Select and write an idiomatic expression on the title page.<br>3. Lightly sketch first and last images. Include only necessary details.<br>4. Sketch intermediary images on other pages to take viewer sequentially from initial picture to final one. |

What the Dickens?
Artist: Gene Mater
2 1/2" x 12"
Collection of the artist.

| | K-2 | 3-4 | 5-6 |
|---|---|---|---|
| **Process: Session 2** 45-60 min | **Illustrate books** 3. Illustrate the three events in detail. Show the setting, characters, and other information necessary to understand what happened. 4. Decorate the front and back covers as well with the book title, student name, and other information and designs. | **Design posters** 3. Transfer sketch to white drawing paper or poster board. Add title. Use bold markers for strong visibility. Outline title with a second color to provide contrast. 4. Take turns drawing various plants and animals native to the ecosystem in the appropriate sequential order on the food chain. Refer to research materials for accurate details. 5. Label plants and animals with scientifically correct names. | **Refine images** 5. Outline images. Add color if desired. 6. Lay pages out to review visual effect. When satisfied, arrange in a sequential pile with title page on top. Fasten securely with staples. 7. Flip through pages to observe sequential movement. |
| **Process: Session 3** 30-45 min. | **Share stories** 5. Students share stories with classmates. Rely on accordion books to assure sequential retellings. | **Share and compare data** 6. Groups give oral presentations using posters as visual aids. 7. Compare ecosystems among groups. What are some similarities and differences? | **Share and compare flipbooks** 8. Encourage classmates to share flipbooks. Discuss images. What techniques are most effective? |
| **Assessment** | • Is book neatly folded into three sequentially numbered pages? • Does each page include a sentence that accurately describes the event? • Are illustrations detailed and colorful? | • Did students work cooperatively to collect data? • Is poster design bold and well balanced? • Do poster details show evidence of careful research? • Is food web sequentially correct? | • Is an idiomatic expression clearly written on front cover? • Do images relate directly to the expression? Are they simply and clearly drawn? • Does sequential progression from first to last image create an illusion of movement? |
| | • Ask students to reflect on this lesson and write a DREAM statement to summarize the most important things they learned. | | |
| **Extensions** | Young children and those with special needs may need help with accordion folds. Artistically talented students may wish to include several additional pages. Practice playing games using various sequencing patterns. | Encourage students with strong leadership skills to provide opportunities for all students (especially those with special needs) to contribute to group effort. Visit a local park to observe a local ecosystem. Invite students to diagram food chains for their favorite meals. | Students who are native speakers of other languages and some students with special needs may require help interpreting idiomatic expressions. Ask gifted students to research early filmmaking or other types of visual illusions. Invite an ophthalmologist to explain how the eye and brain work to create the illusion of movement. |

Artwork by students from
St. John Neumann School,
Palmerton, Pennsylvania.
Teacher: Paula Zelienka

Crayola Dream~Makers®
Building fun and creativity into standards-based learning

# Here Is Looking at You!

## Objectives

Students spell, define, and use new vocabulary words to describe human emotions that are commonly conveyed by facial expressions.

Students represent at least one of those vocabulary words in expressive self-portraits that use art elements and principles such as line, shape, color, texture, pattern, balance, and movement.

## Multiple Intelligences

Bodily-kinesthetic
Interpersonal
Intrapersonal
Linguistic

## What Does It Mean?

**Art elements:** basic attributes such as line, shape, color, form, and texture that create a work of art

**Art principles:** use of art elements to achieve balance, repetition/rhythm/pattern, unity, contrast, variety, proportion, emphasis, and movement in a work of art

**Illuminate:** make resplendent by decorating letters, pages, paragraphs, or borders with colors and gold or silver as was done in the Middle Ages

**Self-portrait:** representation of an individual made by that individual

## National Standards

**Visual Arts Standard #1**
Understanding and applying media, techniques, and processes

**Visual Arts Standard #2**
Using knowledge of structures and functions

**English Language Arts Standard #3**
Students apply a wide range of strategies to comprehend, interpret, evaluate, and appreciate texts. They draw on their prior experience, their interactions with other readers and writers, their knowledge of word meaning and of other texts, their word identification strategies, and their understanding of textual features (e.g., sound-letter correspondence, sentence structure, context, graphics).

**English Language Arts Standard #4**
Students adjust their use of spoken, written, and visual language (e.g., conventions, style, vocabulary) to communicate effectively with a variety of audiences and for different purposes.

## Background Information

Artists often use portraits to communicate messages. Viewers of portraits can learn much about a person's status in society, personality, and interests based on what the subjects are wearing, what they are doing, and their body language and facial expressions. Portraits give insight into the life portrayed.

Two famous portrait artists are the Dutch Renaissance painter, Rembrandt van Rijn, and Gilbert Stuart, who gained fame as an early artist in the United States. Chuck Close is a contemporary artist who is famous for his very large portraits of people.

## Resources

*Alexander and the Terrible, Horrible, No Good, Very Bad Day*
by Judith Viorst
Young children readily identify with Alexander's fluctuating emotions. Experiment with facial expressions reflecting his many moods.

*Drawing Portraits* by Douglas R. Graves
Step-by-step instructions in portrait drawing, helpful to students of all ages. Focuses on individual features (eyes, nose, mouth) and includes sample portraits of a variety of models.

*Helen Keller: Courage in the Dark* by Joanna Hurwitz
Introduces young children to the important role facial expressions play in communicating emotions.

*Helen Keller: Rebellious Spirit* by Laurie Lawlor
Award-winning book for older elementary students. Captures interest and contributes to awareness of how facial expressions communicate emotions.

## Vocabulary List

*Use this list to explore new vocabulary, create idea webs, or brainstorm related subjects.*

Angry
  Enraged
  Furious
  Irate
Communicate
Cross-hatching
Emotions
  Feelings
  Moods
Happy
  Ecstatic
  Serene
Illuminate
Pattern
Portrait
  Self-portrait
Proud
  Glowing

Sad
  Devastated
  Morose
Shape
Shy
  Bashful
  Timid
Surprised
  Astounded
  Awed

Texture
Vain
  Arrogant
  Conceited
  Egotistical
  Haughty
Worried
  Anxious
  Fearful
  Terrified

Drawing, Portrait of a Gentleman
1833
Worcester Twp., Montgomery Co.
Hand-drawn and colored
on wove paper
32 x 20.5 cm; 12 1/2 x 8 in.
Collection of the Schwenkfelder
Library & Heritage Center
Pennsburg, Pennsylvania.

Artwork by students from
St. John Neumann School,
Palmerton, Pennsylvania.
Teacher: Paula Zelienka

| | K-2 | 3-4 | 5-6 |
|---|---|---|---|
| **Suggested Preparation and Discussion** | Display reproductions of portraits that reflect a variety of periods, styles, and emotional expressions. Include some sculptures (busts) if possible. | | |
| | Read picture books that include expressively illustrated characters. Ask students to think about what emotions the characters in the books feel. Notice how the illustrations portray these emotions.<br><br>Discuss how facial expressions communicate thoughts and feelings to others. | Read and discuss fiction and non-fiction books that focus on specific characters such as Helen Keller. Discuss how Helen often touched people's faces to understand what they were feeling.<br><br>Talk about the variety of human emotions and the many words we have to describe them. Describe how facial expressions reflect these emotions. | |
| | Examine and study the illustrations and portraits. Ask students to share their thoughts on the definition of the word *portrait*. Provide background knowledge on portraits.<br><br>Demonstrate how to use shapes when drawing faces. | | |

# Here Is Looking at You!

| | K-2 | 3-4 | 5-6 |
|---|---|---|---|
| **Crayola® Supplies** | • Colored Pencils  • Crayons  • School Glue | | • Markers<br>• Model Magic® or Air-Dry Clay<br>• Paint Brushes<br>• Tempera Paint and/or Watercolors |
| **Other Materials** | • Index cards  • White drawing paper | | |
| | • Construction paper<br>• Unbreakable mirrors | • Mirrors  • Thesauruses | |
| **Set-up/Tips** | | | • The sculpting process may take several days. Cover Air-Dry Clay with plastic to keep material moist. Mist surfaces lightly with water to add more clay.<br>• Attach fresh Model Magic directly to dry compound with glue.<br>• Air-Dry Clay is dry in 3 days. Model Magic sculptures air-dry in 24 hours. |
| **Process: Session 1 20-30 min.** | **Select words to describe emotions**<br>1. Think together about facial expressions such as happy, sad, excited, and confused.<br>2. In mirrors, students study their own facial features as they express these emotions.<br>3. Discuss the ways faces change to reflect feelings. | **Select words to describe emotions**<br>1. Working together, make a list of seven or eight common emotions. Think of alternative words to describe these emotions. Use a thesaurus to add to the list.<br>2. Discuss fine shades of meaning among similar words.<br>3. Students work with partners to experiment with various facial expressions. What parts of the face change? | |
| | 4. Students select one emotion (K-2, 5-6) or three emotions (3-4). On index cards, write a word that describes the emotion. Illuminate and decorate the word with colors, shapes, lines, textures, and/or patterns reflective of the emotion(s). | | |
| **Process: Session 2 20-30 min.** | **Draw self-portraits to show an emotion**<br>5. Review basic portrait-drawing techniques. Start with an egg shape or oval for the head. Then lightly draw the general shape of eyes, nose, and mouth in ways that express the chosen emotion.<br>6. Add neck and shoulders. Encourage children to maintain relative proportions. Refer to mirror images or partner's face as needed. | **Start a series of portraits that show a variety of emotions**<br>5. Recall how to draw a portrait.<br>6. Draw a self-portrait with a specific expression representing the emotion chosen in Session 1. | **Create expressive 3-D sculptures**<br>5. Using Model Magic or Air-Dry Clay compound, students create expressive 3-D portraits of themselves. Start with a disk about the size of an out-stretched hand and about 1/2" thick.<br>6. Build up the surface with additional compound to create low-relief facial features including eyes, lips, nose, forehead, cheeks, and chin.<br>7. Add expressive details such as wrinkles and exaggerated features. Use a mirror when necessary. |

**Face Mask**
2001
Artist unknown
Carved wood
6 1/2" x 4 3/8" x 2 1/2"
Indonesia
Private Collection.

| | K-2 | 3-4 | 5-6 |
|---|---|---|---|
| **Process: Session 3** 20-30 min. | 7. Color portraits. Demonstrate various shading, color mixing, and cross-hatching techniques appropriate to children's skill levels.<br><br>8. Cut small, notched triangles from black construction paper to look like photo mounting corners. Glue triangles to corners of portraits.<br><br>9. Glue portraits to colored construction paper backgrounds, leaving room at the bottom to attach the index card with the word describing the illustrated emotion. Air-dry the glue. | 7. Repeat the process choosing a new emotion and expression. Make at least 3 drawings to complete the series. | 8. Add hair, ears, and a neck. See tips for joining surfaces.<br><br>9. Talk about how working with modeling compound helps students understand the three-dimensional qualities of a face. Correlate this to the way Helen Keller felt faces to understand people in her world. |
| **Process: Session 4** 20-30 min. | 10. Display portraits on a classroom bulletin board or in a class album. | 8. Color the portraits. Use shading, color mixing, and cross-hatching techniques.<br><br>9. Mount portraits in a series, leaving room at the bottom to attach the index cards with the words describing the illustrated emotions. Air-dry the glue.<br><br>10. Display portraits on a classroom bulletin board or in a class album. | 10. Paint portrait sculptures. Avoid using excessive amounts of water on Air-Dry Clay because the clay will become soft and loose its shape. Air-dry sculptures. |
| **Process: Session 5** 20-30 min. | | | 11. Add details with markers.<br><br>12. Display portraits with index cards describing illustrated emotion. |
| **Assessment** | • Does the selected word describe the chosen emotion? Do the portrait's details convey that emotion? | colspan• Does the selected word indicate a "stretch" by the student to use new vocabulary to describe human emotions? Does the portrait provide adequate visual cues to convey the intended emotion? | |

• Ask students to reflect on this lesson and write a DREAM statement to summarize the most important things they learned.

**Extensions**

Some students with learning disabilities may find it more comfortable to work with magazine pictures of faces as their models.

Cover the words on the drawings. Ask students to identify what emotion is illustrated in each portrait. Talk about what details in the picture help reveal the emotion.

In small groups, develop "dictionaries" of words that are used to describe a single emotion.

Illustrate them with drawings or a collage of printed images.

Write one-act plays in which events trigger the emotions depicted. How can these emotions be dealt with in a positive manner? Role-play several possible outcomes.

Gifted students could research famous portraits that reflect emotion, write biographies about the artist and individual portrayed, and explain the circumstances surrounding creation of the portrait.

Face Mask
Circa 1900s, Artist unknown
Carved and hand-painted wood
6 3/8" x 6 1/2" x 3"
Tibet
Private Collection.

Face Mask
2000, Artist unknown
Carved and stained wood
4 3/8" x 6" x 3"
Osaka, Japan
Private Collection.

# Words to Draw On

## Objectives

Students identify challenging new vocabulary words and/or parts of speech from a variety of texts.

Students select, illustrate, and illuminate new vocabulary words to use as visual study aids.

## Multiple Intelligences

Linguistic
Logical-mathematical

## What Does It Mean?

**Etymology:** study of words

**Illuminate:** make resplendent by decorating letters, pages, paragraphs, or borders with colors and gold or silver as was done in the Middle Ages

**Visual symbols:** commonly understood representations of ideas, such a heart meaning love

**Visualize:** process of recalling or imagining mental pictures

## National Standards

**Visual Arts Standard #1**
Understanding and applying media, techniques, and processes

**Visual Arts Standard #6**
Making connections between visual arts and other disciplines.

**English Language Arts Standard #3**
Students apply a wide range of strategies to comprehend, interpret, evaluate, and appreciate texts. They draw on their prior experience, their interactions with other readers and writers, their knowledge of word meaning and of other texts, their word identification strategies, and their understanding of textual features (e.g., sound-letter correspondence, sentence structure, context, graphics).

**English Language Arts Standard #12**
Students use spoken, written, and visual language to accomplish their own purposes (e.g., for learning, enjoyment, persuasion, and the exchange of information).

## Background Information

Years ago, religious leaders taught young children lessons by using brightly colored windows of stained glass that contained images of people, places and things. The images helped children understand the stories or messages the leaders were trying to teach. Drawing pictures of people, places, and things often helps children communicate before they are able to read text. For students who have difficulty learning to read or who are learning a second language, it is especially important that pictures tell the same story as the words. This strengthens children's understanding of the story and the text.

As children learn about language patterns, being able to visualize grammatical structures helps with comprehension. Likewise, in learning vocabulary, being able to visually trace the origin of one word improves students' word attack skills when faced with similar but new words.

## Resources

*Beyond Words: A Guide to Drawing Out Ideas*
by Milly Sonneman
Inspires adults as well as children. Graphically shows students how to connect words and ideas for an audience.

*Visual Thinking: Tools for Mapping Your Ideas*
by Nancy Margulies and Christine Valenza
Shows how to use visual symbols as a means of thinking. Techniques provide helpful tools for improving reading comprehension as well as note taking, problem solving, and study skills. Provides instruction in the creation of visual aids such as mindscapes and mind maps.

*www.etymonline.com*
Information on Greek and Latin word origins as well as other interesting history of words.

## Vocabulary List

*Use this list to explore new vocabulary, create idea webs, or brainstorm related subjects.*

- Prepositions

| About | In | Over |
|-------|-----|------|
| Around | Into | To |
| Behind | Near | Under |
| Between | On | With |

- Words with Greek and Latin origins

| Arachnophobia | Hydroplane | Polychromatic |
|---------------|------------|---------------|
| Astronaut | Metropolis | Submarine |
| Centipede | Microscope | Symmetrical |
| Compass | Monocle | Telephone |

- Other vocabulary
  Borders
  Congruent
  Decorative
  Etymology
  Illuminate
  Parts of speech
  Visual symbols

Artwork by students from Northeast Elementary School, Vernon, Connecticut.
Teacher: Keith Giard

Artwork by students from
Mt. Prospect Elementary School,
Basking Ridge, New Jersey.
Teacher: Susan Bivona

A plane flew over a cloud
around
under
through

Astro — star or other heavenly body [<Greek< astron star]

Astronaut = pilot or member of the crew of a space craft

Artwork by students
from St. John Neumann School,
Palmerton, Pennsylvania.
Teacher: Paula Zelienka

Crayola **Dream~Makers**
Building fun and creativity into standards-based learning

# Words to Draw On

| | K-2 | 3-4 | 5-6 |
|---|---|---|---|
| **Suggested Preparation and Discussion** | Display picture books and other samples of graphic arts where text is congruent with illustrations. Gather dictionaries to provide etymologies for words. Display sample art projects to inspire children's creativity. | | |
| | With children, list challenging new vocabulary words from books that they have looked at or read recently. Discuss definitions of these words. | Write a sentence containing a prepositional phrase. Ask students to identify the preposition. Explain that "anything a plane can do to a cloud is a preposition." Work together to list other prepositions.<br><br>Demonstrate how visual images can be used as a study aid by drawing simple pictures illustrating various prepositional phrases relating to a plane and a cloud (such as over the cloud and through a cloud). | Write the word *etymology* along with several common words with Greek or Latin origins (such as astronaut or automobile).<br><br>Ask what students know about new words being added to a language to accommodate new inventions or ideas. Suggest they interview older family members. Ask what words have been added to the language in their lifetimes.<br><br>Define *etymology* and trace the origin of at least one word. |
| **Crayola® Supplies** | • Colored Pencils    • Washable Markers | | |
| **Other Materials** | • Drawing paper    • White paper | | |
| **Process: Session 1 20-30 min.** | **Compare text and illustrations**<br>1. Read a picture book without showing the illustrations. Students imagine how an artist might illustrate the story. Compare the actual illustrations with their own ideas.<br>2. Look at examples of illuminated texts in the classroom display. Discuss how a word within a sentence could be illuminated to reflect its meaning. | **Illuminate a phrase**<br>1. Write a sentence that contains a prepositional phrase.<br>2. Illustrate key words in the phrase. Follow examples from the classroom display of graphic arts and illuminated texts.<br>3. Create decorative borders that visually reflect the theme as expressed in words. | **Research word origins**<br>1. Using dictionaries or Web resources, research the origins of words with Greek or Latin roots.<br>2. Review the visual displays in the classroom. Discuss how illustrations can be used to extend and enhance information.<br>3. Select one of the researched words. Using classroom examples of textual graphics as models, write the word, its definition, and its etymology on drawing paper. |

**Vessel With Decorative Border**
Circa 1900s
Artist unknown
Terra cotta clay with white slip decoration
8 1/2" x 22 1/2" x 9"
Turkey
Private Collection.

**Cuba Cloth Design With Decorative Pattern**
Circa 1900s
Artist unknown
Hand dyed and woven jute
17" x 15 1/2"
Zaire, Africa
Private Collection.

| | K-2 | 3-4 | 5-6 |
|---|---|---|---|
| **Process: Session 2** 20-30 min. | **Illustrate vocabulary word** 3. Think about the meaning of new vocabulary words. Write a sentence that contains two or more of these words on drawing paper. 4. Illustrate one of the words within the sentence. Create a decorative border that continues the theme. | **Illustrate sentence** 4. On a separate paper, illustrate the entire sentence with an emphasis on the image conveyed by the prepositional phrase. | **Illustrate etymology of word** 4. On separate paper, illustrate the chosen word with details related to its etymology. For example, an astronaut might be pictured in a starry setting. |
| **Process: Session 3** 20-30 min. | **Illustrate sentence** 5. On a second sheet of paper, draw a picture of the person, place, thing, or idea that the sentence is about. Then add details to illustrate the meaning of the entire sentence. 6. Compare original drawings with the illuminated sentences. | **Match prepositional phrases to illustrations** 5. Arrange student work in two separate piles. Students identify the prepositional phrases in each. 6. Challenge students to match sentences with illustrations. Reflect on why some were more difficult than others to match. | **Build vocabulary** 5. Classmates share their projects as a study aid for learning new vocabulary. |
| **Assessment** | • Do illustrations focus on the main noun in the accompanying sentence? • How well do details match the context of the sentence? • Do drawings accurately reflect the meaning of the words? | • Students accurately identify prepositional phrases within their sentences. • Students illustrate sentences with details that visually convey their meanings. • Students are engaged in the process of matching sentences with illustrations. | • Students accurately trace the origin of a word and prepare an illustrated poster that includes the word, its definition, and its etymology as well as visual cues to its Greek or Latin origin. |
| | • Ask students to reflect on this lesson and write a DREAM statement to summarize the most important things they learned. | | |
| **Extensions** | Children practice decoding skills by reading classmates' sentences aloud, using illustrations as context clues to help with difficult words. Use storytelling as the basis for children's illustrations of scenes, characters, and settings. Reflect on how differently children imagine the same story. Students compare books they read with movies based on the books. What was similar? Different? Which did they prefer? Why? | Integrate kinesthetic and spatial intelligence with linguistic intelligence, especially for students with special needs. Students use Crayola® Model Magic® compound to sculpt two objects that appear in a prepositional phrase such as a plane and a cloud. Students use these to demonstrate the concept of the prepositional phrase. (The plane flies *to* the cloud, *around* the cloud, or *over* the cloud, for example.) In a newspaper, search for prepositional phrases. Mark them with color to show how extensively they are used. Challenge students to write poetry or musical lyrics using as many different prepositions as possible. | Provide a list of advanced vocabulary words with Greek or Latin word parts (such as *polypod* or *hydrophone*). Challenge students to define the words based on what they learned from this lesson. Ask gifted students to work in small groups to invent new words with Greek or Latin roots. Write the words and their meanings on cards. Mix the cards with those containing similar words already in the dictionary. Exchange cards with another group. Which team can most accurately identify the invented vocabulary? |

Crayola Dream~Makers®
Building fun and creativity into standards-based learning

## Objectives

Students identify challenging vocabulary words from fiction or non-fiction literature and include the words along with symbols to create a class or team mural.

Students in grades 3 to 6 identify English idioms or figurative language that can be represented by visual symbols and then create individual paintings that will becomes sections of a large class mural.

Students design, create, and discuss individual, class, or team murals that include text and illustration.

## Multiple Intelligences

| Bodily-kinesthetic | Spatial |
| Linguistic | |

## National Standards

| **Visual Arts Standard #3** Choosing and evaluating a range of subject matter, symbols and ideas | *Grades K-4* **English Language Arts Standard #3** Students apply a wide range of strategies to comprehend, interpret, evaluate and appreciate texts. They draw on their prior experience, their interactions with other readers and writers, their knowledge of word meaning and of other texts, their word identification strategies, and their understanding of textual features (e.g., sound-letter correspondence, sentence structure, context, graphics). *Grades 5-6* **English Language Arts Standard #6** Students apply knowledge of language structure, language conventions (e.g., spelling and punctuation), media techniques, figurative language, and genre to create, critique, and discuss print and non-print texts. *Students Learning English as a Second Language* **English Language Arts Standard #10** Students whose first language is not English make use of their first language to develop competency in the English language arts and to develop understanding of content across the curriculum. |
|---|---|

## Background Information

A mural is typically a larger-than-life work of art painted directly on a wall or ceiling. Some of the oldest known murals are the cave paintings of Lascaux. These 15,000- to 17,000-year-old paintings, discovered in southern France in 1840, depict visual symbols of animals and symbols related to humans such as hands.

Italian frescoes are often unified with a story that depicts people, places, and things. Michelangelo created the Sistine Chapel fresco during the Renaissance. Thousands of visitors have admired his interpretation of the Biblical creation that visually depicts people, places, and things.

During the 20th century Diego Rivera created frescos and murals in both Mexico and the United States. Some of Rivera's American murals unify story through the symbols, and images of people, places, and events that are included in the work.

Today Philadelphia has more murals than any other city in the world thanks to the work of Jane Golden and her Mural Arts Project. What began as an anti-graffiti campaign has since grown into an arts program for youth throughout the city.

## Resources

*Diego* by Jonah and Jeannette Winter
Picture book biography of Diego Rivera. Excellent introduction to mural arts for ages 4 to 8. English and Spanish text is easy to read. Colorful borders filled with Mexican folk art motifs.

*Philadelphia Murals and the Stories They Tell*
by Jane Golden and Robin Rice
For readers of all ages. Fascinating story of Golden's successful and inspiring anti-graffiti program. Photos of larger-than-life community murals that convey messages of pride, hope, and history.

*Super Silly Sayings That Are Over Your Head: A Children's Illustrated Book of Idioms* by Catherine Snodgrass
Entertaining guide to English idioms. Clarifies mysteries of the language for ESL students. Assists elementary students and children with certain forms of autism as they struggle to understand the difference between literal and figurative language.

*Teaching Reading and Writing With Word Walls*
by Janiel Wagstaff
For elementary teachers. Describes many different kinds of word walls and related lessons.

## Vocabulary List

*Select vocabulary directly related to students' current reading. Look for words that can be easily illustrated such as concrete nouns, adjectives, and active verbs. Use this list to explore new vocabulary, create idea webs, or brainstorm related subjects.*

- Art vocabulary

| Background | Graffiti | Theme |
| Border | Mural | Unity |
| Enlarge | Reproduction | |
| Foreground | Symbol | |

- Figurative language

| Hyperbole | Metaphor | Oxymoron |
| Idiom | Onomatopoeia | Simile |

## What Does It Mean?

**Figurative language:** words not intended to be taken literally

**Fresco:** art technique of painting, originally on a moist, plaster surface with colors ground up in water or a limewater mixture

**Idioms:** style of artistic expression characteristic of a particular individual, culture, or language

**Onomatopoeia:** rhetorical use of words that imitate natural sounds

**Unified mural:** a large display in which all the parts fit a theme or work as a whole unit

**Crayola**

**Dream~Makers®**
Building fun and creativity into standards-based learning

|  | K-2 | 3-4 | 5-6 |
|---|---|---|---|
| **Suggested Preparation and Discussion** | Display reproductions of various murals. Collaborate with the art teacher to show students how murals are made.<br><br>With students, make word cards that name objects in murals shown.<br><br>Identify and prepare space to use as a word wall (a type of mural). Make word cards with definitions on the card backs. Add cards with words essential to sentence structure (pronouns, articles, prepositions). Post cards in a prominent location on the word wall. Discuss words and murals. | Research famous muralists, such as Diego Rivera, and the works they created. Display samples of several types of murals. Talk about elements of mural design such as theme and unity.<br><br>Create a sample section of an "idiom" mural that includes symbols and words. Discuss the definition of figurative language.<br><br>Invite students to examine the murals on display with questions such as, Why do people make murals? Where are murals in our community? Who made them? What are they about?<br><br>Explain that students will make murals to help others understand oddities in the English language such as figurative language. Together, make a list of idioms such as "It's raining cats and dogs," or "I have a frog in my throat." | |
| **Crayola® Supplies** | • Colored Pencils • Markers • Paint Brushes • Scissors • Tempera Paints | | |
| **Other Materials** | • Index cards | • Oak tag | |
| | • Masking tape • Recycled newspaper • Rolled craft paper • Water containers • White paper | | |
| **Set-up/Tips** | • To enlarge sketches, make photocopy transparencies of them. Use an overhead projector to show the picture on craft paper taped to a wall. Outline the enlarged sketch. | | |
| **Process: Session 1**<br><br>Grades K-2<br>20-30 min.<br><br>Grades 3-6<br>45-60 min. | **Develop vocabulary**<br>1. Students select words from assigned readings and make word cards that can be arranged in a meaningful sentence.<br>2. Discuss and share ideas for illustrating sentences. What pictures could represent the words? Sketch illustrations that reflect sentences.<br>3. Identify a unifying theme for a class word mural. Talk about what symbols represent words effectively. Show examples of illustrations in picture books.<br>4. Discuss how to unify the images on the mural with a common theme, color, background, border, or other technique. What will be in the foreground? Plan to fill the entire space! | **Correlate idioms with images**<br>1. Students choose partners. Each pair chooses an idiom to represent with visual symbols.<br>2. Cut a strip of oak tag and write the idiom on it in bold, colorful letters.<br>3. One member of the pair sketches a literal translation of the idiom in symbols. The other partner sketches a figurative meaning.<br>4. Partners discuss their results with each other. | **Correlate metaphor with images**<br>1. Students research the definition of metaphor and discuss their findings.<br>2. Vote to select one class metaphor, such as "All the world is a stage."<br>3. Each classmate draws a picture that reflects the metaphor.<br>4. Discuss the drawings to determine what parts of each drawing could be included in a large class mural. Make sure all students are represented in the design! |

Olive Tree Mural
Artist: Dusty Kramer
Portfolio acrylic paint on stucco wall
12' x 20'
Napa, California
Collection of Linda Parzych
and Bob Fowles.
Photograph: R. De Long

| | K-2 | 3-4 | 5-6 |
|---|---|---|---|
| **Process: Session 2 45-60 min.** | **Design a mural** 5. Create transparencies of sketches. Project sections on mural paper. Move images to various locations to decide on the best position on the mural. 6. Trace sections on mural paper in final position. Repeat until all students have contributed a section. 7. Add text to unify the sections using block lettering. | | |
| **Process: Session 3 45-60 min.** | **Paint a mural** 8. Lay the mural flat on newspaper. Paint a base coat of color to the shapes and background. 9. Outline the lined areas with bold colors! Contrasting colors help distinguish and separate spaces in the design. Fill the mural with color. Air-dry the paint. | | |
| **Process: Session 4 20-30 min.** | **Discuss text and illustrations** 10. Discuss the mural. What vocabulary images are recognizable? What additional details are shown? 11. Students write sentences about the mural using newly learned words. 12. Students orally share their sentences with the class. | **Discuss mural** 10. Are any additional symbols or design elements needed to convey the idea of idioms in the mural design? Add them. 11. Invite a group of younger students and/or families who are learning English to view the mural. Students discuss their idioms and images and answer any questions. | **Discuss mural** 10. Examine the work in progress to see if any additional design elements will help convey the idea of the metaphor. Add last-minute design adjustments as needed. |
| **Assessment** | • Can students read the target words on the mural as well as the sentences they wrote? • Do the images on the mural accurately reflect the meanings of the words? | • Challenge pairs of students to check the artwork of other pairs to see if the idea of literal and figurative has been achieved in the design work. • Ask students to orally debate why artwork does or does not meet the lesson objective so they can intelligently talk to visitors who come to class. | • Ask students to write a paragraph that explains how the mural illustrates the metaphor that was illustrated in the mural. • Post all the writings next to the mural design for school community members to read. |
| | • Is the mural unified with a theme and/or the use of color and design? • Ask students to reflect on this lesson and write a DREAM statement to summarize the most important things they learned. | | |
| **Extensions** | Encourage children to continue making colorful word cards throughout the year, posting them on significant objects in the classroom and at home to enhance sight-reading vocabulary. Set aside space for a word wall where students write and illustrate new words throughout the year. Change paper periodically. The kinesthetic act of writing words and images on the wall is especially valuable for students with a variety of learning differences. | As a community service project, invite students to make illustrated idiom books to give to students or families who are learning English. Students with social and verbal talents might work one on one with students who are learning English or whose special needs make it difficult for them to understand the concept of figurative language. | Create a class book that includes metaphors with text and illustration. Work with a local business to see if the class can recreate the mural in a public space within the community. Write press releases to send to the media along with digital images of the metaphor mural to get coverage about the mural project. Invite local business people and governmental officials to attend a mural dedication. |
| | Examine murals in the community. Research the community mural artist(s) and how the mural was commissioned and executed. Work with an artist in residence to prepare a mural for display in a public building. | | |

Crayola

**Dream~Makers®**
Building fun and creativity into standards-based learning

# Talented Talkers: Puppets With Speech Bubbles

## Objectives

Students work cooperatively in small groups to write mini-play dialogs that expand their spoken and written vocabulary based on assigned fiction and non-fiction literary assignments.

Students understand the logic of thinking, writing, and performing actions in sequence in order to convey ideas effectively to others.

Students create hand puppets with dialog speech bubbles and perform mini-plays before an audience.

Students enrich their vocabulary and writing skills.

## Multiple Intelligences

| Bodily-kinesthetic | Linguistic |
| --- | --- |
| Interpersonal | |

## National Standards

| Visual Arts Standard #6<br>Making connections between visual arts and other disciplines | **English Language Arts Standard #4**<br>Students adjust their use of spoken, written, and visual language (e.g., conventions, style, vocabulary) to communicate effectively with a variety of audiences and for different purposes.<br>**English Language Arts Standard #11**<br>Students participate as knowledgeable, reflective, creative, and critical members of a variety of literacy communities.<br>**English Language Arts Standard #12**<br>Students use spoken, written, and visual language to accomplish their own purposes (e.g., for learning, enjoyment, persuasion, and the exchange of information).<br>*Grades 5-6*<br>**English Language Arts Standard #2**<br>Students read a wide range of literature from many periods in many genres to build an understanding of the many dimensions (e.g., philosophical, ethical, aesthetic) of human experience.<br>**English Language Arts Standard #3**<br>Students apply a wide range of strategies to comprehend, interpret, evaluate, and appreciate texts. They draw on their prior experience, their interactions with other readers and writers, their knowledge of word meaning and of other texts, their word identification strategies, and their understanding of textual features (e.g., sound-letter correspondence, sentence structure, context, graphics). |

## Background Information

Puppets are an old form of art and entertainment. Ancient puppets have been discovered in the Americas, the Czech Republic, and other countries around the world. Multiple cultures use puppets for rituals, ceremonies, processions, storytelling, children's toys, and entertainment. Some countries perform entire plays using puppets without any spoken words.

Puppets also play a valuable role in education. They are a nonthreatening vehicle for communication and provide opportunities for children to explore new ideas and vocabulary. When staff at the University of London and Manchester Metropolitan University conducted a joint study of puppetry in science classrooms, they discovered that the percentage of time children spent on conversation involving reasoning exceeded practical talk ("Please pass the scissors") when children used puppets to conduct their experiments. For more information, see *www.puppetsproject.com/documents/puppets-t-earth-sci06.doc*.

## Resources

*Matilda* by Roald Dahl
From the terrible Trunchbull to gentle Miss Honey, strongly delineated characters make interesting puppets. Third and fourth grade students also will be inspired by Matilda's love of learning.

*Puppets Around the World* by Meryl Doney
Large color photographs and clear diagrams and directions. An excellent resource for all elementary school puppet makers.

*The American Heritage Picture Word Book* by the editors of the American Heritage Dictionaries
Introduction to vocabulary study. Centers on scenes of interest to young children: playground, ocean, outer space. Labeled objects, activities, and people fill each page.

*The Phantom Tollbooth* by Norton Juster
Fantasy adventure for older elementary students in which word play predominates. Fascinating, unusual characters provide rich material for puppet making.

## Vocabulary List

*Use this list to explore new vocabulary, create idea webs, or brainstorm related subjects.*

Blocking
Characterization
Clarity
Costume
Dialog
Enunciation
Expressive
Facial features
Mobility
Performance
Precise
Pronunciation
Puppetry
Role
Sculpt
Set design
Vivid

Artwork by students from St. Theresa Elementary School, Hellertown, Pennsylvania.

## What Does It Mean?

**Marionette:** puppet manipulated from above by strings attached to its jointed limbs

**Puppet:** representation of a human, animal or other being, typically manipulated by the hand, rod, or wire

Artwork by students from
Mt. Prospect Elementary School,
Basking Ridge, New Jersey.
Teacher: Nancy Knutsen

| | K-2 | 3-4 | 5-6 |
|---|---|---|---|
| **Suggested Preparation and Discussion** | Tailor this lesson to build on a classroom field experience such as a visit to a garden center, aquarium, or hardware store. Check with the site manager to see if children are allowed to draw on location.<br><br>Design and display a vocabulary poster that contains specific words and definitions that relate to the visit. Leave space for additional words. For example, if the class visits a garden center, they might list lilies of the valley, purple iris, or boxwood hedge (rather than flowers and bushes). Point out how specific words help listeners see a vivid picture in their minds and imagine they can smell the fragrances. | Assemble fiction and non-fiction books into a library for children to look at and read. Include books with interesting characters and rich vocabulary.<br><br>Schedule reading time, discussion time, script writing time, and performance time for the class so they can develop and perform mini-plays relative to assigned readings.<br><br>Create sample puppets and speech bubbles. Explain how to develop a script that has a sequence of events and uses descriptive words. Create a sample script to read with students.<br><br>Display various types of puppets. | |
| | Explain to students that they will create puppet characters and write a script about their field experience (K-2) or a story scene (3-6) to present to their classmates.<br>Display examples of paper bag character puppets. | | |
| **Crayola® Supplies** | • Colored Pencils   • Markers   • Model Magic®   • School Glue   • Scissors | | |
| | • Paint Brushes (optional)<br>• Watercolors (optional) | | |

# Talented Talkers: Puppets With Speech Bubbles

| | K-2 | 3-4 | 5-6 |
|---|---|---|---|
| **Other Materials** | • Oak tag • White paper | | |
| | • Construction paper<br>• Decorative craft materials such as chenille stems or feathers<br>• Modeling tools such as plastic dinner knives, craft sticks, and toothpicks<br>• Paper lunch bags • Recycled newspaper • Water containers (optional) | | • Recycled cardboard boxes<br>• Theater face make up (optional)<br>• White drawing paper |
| **Set-up/Tips** | • Use masking tape loops to attach speech bubbles to puppet mouths. Tape can easily be removed to change bubbles during dialogue. | | |
| | • Cover painting surface with newspaper. | | • Ask families to help locate clothing for costumes and other props. |
| **Process: Session 1**<br>30-45 min. or more | **Research dialogue**<br>1. Ask students to choose a real or imagined character from a school field experience. Suggest classmates, chaperones, a tour guide, or something they saw.<br>2. Students add words they heard during their trip to the class word poster. Select one word for creating a puppet with speech bubbles.<br>3. In small groups, students decide how their puppets will interact with each other using dialog.<br>4. Write dialog for puppets, using at least one specific, new vocabulary word per puppet. | **Write script**<br>1. Teams of three or four students to select one or two interesting scenes from an assigned fiction or non-fiction reading. Determine how many and what kind of characters are needed to portray the scene.<br>2. Write a script with speaking roles for all characters in the scene. Include new vocabulary words for each character in the dialog. If needed, create a character to play the role of an on-stage narrator.<br>3. Roll drawing paper into very tight cylinders. Glue edges and apply pressure until cylinder is dry.<br>4. Cut out large speech bubbles from tag paper. Write dialogue on the bubbles. Decorate the borders of the bubbles. Glue speech bubbles to sticks. | |
| **Process: Session 2**<br><br>Grades K-6<br>30-45. min. or more | **Make speech bubbles**<br>5. Cut oak tag speech bubbles large enough to contain each puppet's dialog. Write text on speech bubble. | | **Make speech bubbles**<br>5. Shape and glue Ping-Pong ball size Model Magic® spheres to one end of the sticks. |
| **Process: Session 3**<br>30-40 min. or more | **Create puppets**<br>6. Design puppet bodies on paper bags, using the bag bottom as the head and the fold as the mouth. Depict clothing, animal body parts and skin, and other details suitable for the character.<br>7. Decorate and cut construction paper pieces as needed for puppet features. For example, older students could wrap paper strips around pencil barrels to curl the paper. Use curled strips for hair, manes, beards, and other features. Glue pieces to the puppet. Air-dry the glue.<br>8. Shape Model Magic® facial features such as eyes, nose, and mouth or other details. Exaggerate features for easy on-stage visibility. Air-dry 24 hours. | | **Design costumes**<br>6. Sketch costumes that correlate to the text in the speech bubbles.<br>7. Find clothing to wear for costumes as planned.<br>8. Collect various accessories such as hats and props that can be used to hallmark the characters. |

**Puppet Mask**
Artist: Bill Skrips
Plaster of Paris, paint
20" x 24" x 18"
Collection of Cara and Bill Skrips.

| | K-2 | 3-4 | 5-6 |
|---|---|---|---|
| **Process:** Session 4 30-45 min. | **Paint facial features (optional)** 9. Paint puppet's facial features with watercolors. Air-dry the paint. | | **Consider face make up** 9. Draw self-portrait plans that include make-up features to match the characters. |
| **Process:** Session 5 30-45 min. | **Assemble puppets** 10. Use fine point markers to add details to facial features. Add chenille stems or other craft materials for decorative touches. Glue pieces in place. 11. Glue speech bubbles extending from mouths. Attach longer scripts to the backs of the puppets. Air-dry the glue. | | **Gather props** 10. Collect essential props to help tell the story to the audience effectively. |
| **Process:** Session 6 30-45 min. | **Rehearse performance** 12. Practice performing with puppets or with their characters before classmates. | | |
| **Process:** Session 7 30-45 min. | **Perform plays** 13. Perform for classmates or others. | | **Perform silent plays** 11. Dress in costumes with makeup as planned. 12. Silently act the roles of characters before an audience. Hold the appropriate speech bubble stick to the mouth when the character delivers dialog. |
| **Assessment** | • Is puppet creatively designed and does it have "character"? | • Does the dialogue match the puppet? Are lines delivered smoothly and in character? • Have audience rate their understanding of the performance. Did the puppet dialogue relate to a scene from the assigned literature reading? Could audience identify characters from the dialog and puppet costume? | • Did students sequence the dialogue of the group of characters so that the silent story made sense? • Ask the audience if they could identify the scene from the assigned literature reading. |

• Does child manipulate puppet well, interacting naturally with other puppets?

• Are speech bubbles filled with dialog? Does the dialogue incorporate new vocabulary in the script? Are spellings correct?

• Ask students to reflect on this lesson and write a DREAM statement to summarize the most important things they learned.

| **Extensions** | Provide spelling assistance and perhaps computers to help students with special needs write their dialog. Make photographic scrapbooks or posters on various curriculum themes. Label with precise vocabulary. | Invite students with a special interest in theater to research one aspect of puppetry or playwriting and present their findings to the class. Shuffle student groupings and challenge groups to create original stories using the new mix of character and performers. Try making other types of puppets including marionettes, shadow puppets, and characters sculpted with Model Magic compound. |
|---|---|---|

Attend a puppet show or invite a puppeteer to perform. Take a "backstage" tour.

Encourage students or families with advanced mechanical or artistic skills to create a puppet theater.

**Stick Puppet**
2004, Artist unknown
Folded and woven palm fronds, string, beads
5" x 6 1/2" x 2 1/2"
Viet Nam
Private Collection.

Crayola **Dream~Makers**
Building fun and creativity into standards-based learning

# Words in the Wind: A Linguistic Balancing Act

## Objectives

Students demonstrate an understanding of structure and function in the physical world as well as the linguistic one.

Students use appropriate parts of speech such as antonyms, homonyms, and syntactical balance.

Students understand the structures and functions of designing and creating a mobile.

## Multiple Intelligences

| Linguistic | Spatial |
| --- | --- |
| Logical-mathematical | |

## National Standards

**Visual Arts Standard #2**
Using knowledge of structures and functions

**Visual Arts Standard #6**
Making connections between visual arts and other disciplines

**English Language Arts Standard #3**
Students apply a wide range of strategies to comprehend, interpret, evaluate, and appreciate texts. They draw on their prior experience, their interactions with other readers and writers, their knowledge of word meaning and of other texts, their word identification strategies, and their understanding of textual features (e.g., sound-letter correspondence, sentence structure, context, graphics).

**English Language Arts Standard #6**
Students apply knowledge of language structure, language conventions (e.g., spelling and punctuation), media techniques, figurative language, and genre to create, critique, and discuss print and nonprint texts.

**English Language Arts Standard #10**
Students whose first language is not English make use of their first language to develop competency in the English language arts and to develop understanding of content across the curriculum.

## Background Information

Alexander Calder (1898-1976) is credited with inventing the mobile as an art form. The mobile was aptly named by another artist, Marcel Duchamps, in 1931. Trained initially as a mechanical engineer, Calder later joined the Art Students League of New York where he studied painting and sculpture. One of his earliest sculptural pieces was a miniature circus made from bent wires, wood, cloth, and cork.

Working with mobiles challenges students to use spatial intelligence as they study balance, movement, and form. These skills play a role in many areas of study including physics, mathematics, and gymnastics as well as art and design. They also are important in linguistics, where students learn to balance structure with function and compare/contrast various words pairs such as homonyms or antonyms.

## Resources

*Antonyms, Synonyms, and Homonyms* by Kim and Robert Rayevsky
An invitation to have fun with words! Linguistic concepts emerge as readers follow the antics of an alien who lands on Earth. Engagingly illustrated. Students in grades 2 to 5 will laugh aloud.

*Eight Ate: A Feast of Homonym Riddles* by Marvin Terba and Giulio Maestro
Each riddle is accompanied by a cartoon illustration hinting at the answer, which is always a pair of homonyms. Humorous introduction to homonyms for 3rd through 6th grades.

*Scholastic Dictionary of Synonyms, Antonyms, and Homonyms* from Scholastic
Excellent reference tool for ages 9 to 12.

*www.nga.gov/exhibitions/calder/realsp/intro.htm*
National Gallery of Art Web site. Includes a virtual tour of work by Alexander Calder and informative text about his mobiles. Excellent resource for teachers.

## Vocabulary List

*Use this list to explore new vocabulary, create idea webs, or brainstorm related subjects.*

- Antonyms

| | |
| --- | --- |
| Big/little | Open/close |
| Black/white | Sleep/wake |
| Give/take | Small/large |
| Hot/cold | Tall/short |
| Laugh/cry | Top/bottom |

- Art terms

| | |
| --- | --- |
| Balance | Movement |
| Baseline | Organic |
| Form | Unity |
| Geometric | Variety |

- Grammar terms

| | |
| --- | --- |
| Adjective | Noun |
| Adverb | Predicate |
| Article | Pronoun |
| Diagram | Subject |
| Direct object | Verb |
| Modifier | |

- Homonyms

| | |
| --- | --- |
| Allowed/aloud | Flea/flee |
| Ate/eight | Flew/flu/flue |
| Blue/blew | One/won |
| Board/bored | Peace/piece |
| Dear/deer | Waist/waste |
| Eye/I | Weak/week |

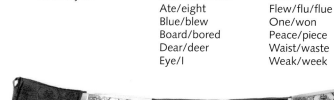

Tibetan Prayer Flags
Printed cotton
6" x 36"
Private Collection.

Artwork by students from
Mt. Prospect Elementary School,
Basking Ridge, New Jersey.
Teacher: Susan Bivona

## What Does It Mean?

**Mobiles:** type of sculpture consisting of carefully equilibrated parts that move in response to air currents

**Organic shapes:** irregular shapes, often like those in nature

**Structure:** 3-dimensional model with several parts

| K-2 | 3-4 | 5-6 |
|---|---|---|

**Suggested Preparation and Discussion**

Display pictures of famous mobiles as well as sample mobiles similar to the project students will make. Introduce the idea of balance as it appears in various subject areas such as physics, mathematics, or gymnastics as well as art. Read together Rayevsky's *Antonyms, Synonyms, and Homonyms* or a similar book that deals with word play.

| K-2 | 3-4 | 5-6 |
|---|---|---|
| Show students two contrasting objects to illustrate the concept of word opposites (big ball, little ball). Ask volunteers to give examples of other word opposite pairs. Write some for all to see.<br><br>Introduce the term *antonym* as appropriate to students' ability levels.<br><br>Tell students they will make mobiles with pairs of antonyms. | Ask volunteers to read homonym pairs aloud and explain differences in meaning.<br><br>Introduce this tongue twister and ask students to identify the homonym pairs: *A flea and a fly in a flue were imprisoned, so what could they do? Said the fly, "Let us flee." Said the flea, "Let us fly." So they flew through a flaw in the flue.* What is the difference between a *flea* and a *fly*? What does *flee* mean? What is a *flue*? What two different meanings does *fly* have in this tongue twister? What homonyms are used?<br><br>Look at sentences where homonyms are misused: *My deer ant cot the flew last weak.* How can students bring that sentence into a more meaningful balance?<br><br>Explain that students will explore the idea of balance in language and art by creating mobiles with pairs of homonyms. | Review grammatical concepts of structure and function for nouns, verbs, adjectives, and adverbs.<br><br>Teach simple, traditional sentence diagramming for subjects, predicates, direct objects, and adjective and adverb modifiers. (Example: My little brother bought two video games yesterday.) Show how the simple subject, simple predicate, and direct object appear on the same baseline while modifiers are placed below the specific words they modify.<br><br>Write and diagram simple, original sentences. Choose one with which to create a balanced verbal mobile. |

Crayola **Dream~Makers**
Building fun and creativity into standards-based learning

# Words in the Wind: A Linguistic Balancing Act

| | K-2 | 3-4 | 5-6 |
|---|---|---|---|
| **Crayola® Supplies** | • Crayons   • Markers   • School Glue   • Scissors | | |
| **Other Materials** | • Hole punch   • Oak tag   • Twigs or dowel sticks   • Yarn or string | | |
| **Set-up/Tips** | • Ask parent volunteers to cut twigs or dowel sticks.<br>• Encourage students to help each other as they assemble mobiles. | | |

**Process: Session 1**
**30-45 min.**

**Create word shapes**

1. Children choose two pairs of antonyms (K-2) or homonyms (3-4). Encourage a wide variety among classmates so final classroom display will include many different word pairs.
2. Cut oak tag into four large organic or geometric shapes. Punch a hole in the top of each one.
3. On the front of each shape write one of the selected words. Make the words easy to read from a distance with techniques such as big letters, bold colors, and wide lines.

**Create word shapes**

1. Students each select a sentence to diagram with a mobile.
2. Cut shapes from oak tag or use index cards, one for each word in the sentence. Punch a hole at the top of each shape.
3. Write one word on each shape. Make the words easy to read from a distance with techniques such as big letters, bold colors, and wide lines.

4. On the back of each shape illustrate the word that appears on the front, emphasizing contrasting characteristics with each antonym pair.

4. At the top of the back of each shape, write a sentence using the homonym that appears on the front in its correct context. Below each sentence, draw an illustration.

4. Illustrate the subject, predicate, direct object, and any other words that can be symbolized.

**Process: Session 2**
**20-30 min.**

**Assemble mobile**

5. Students tie one string to each end of a long stick so the strings hang freely. At the end of each string, tie another stick.
6. From each of these sticks, attach two more strings, one on each end.
7. Tie an antonym (or homonym) shape to the bottom of each string so that antonym (or homonym) pairs are attached to the same stick.
8. Tie a string to the center of the long stick. Use it to suspend the mobile. Experiment with string lengths and position to achieve balance.

**Assemble mobile**

5. Tie three strings (all the same length) to a stick, one in the center and one near each end. Suspend the subject, predicate, and direct object cards, in order, on the strings, much like the baseline of a sentence diagram.
6. Decide which words modify the subject. Punch a row of holes in the bottom of the subject card and hang the modifiers in the order they appear in the original sentence.
7. Identify and hang modifiers for the verb and the direct object in a similar manner. If any words remain (such as articles, pronouns, or modifiers of modifiers as in _very small dog_), hang them where they belong.
8. Tie a string to the top of the stick near the center and use it to suspend the mobile. Experiment with string lengths and position to achieve balance.

Artwork by students from Mt. Prospect Elementary School, Basking Ridge, New Jersey. Teacher: Susan Bivona

| | K-2 | 3-4 | 5-6 |
|---|---|---|---|

**Process:**
**Session 3**
**15-20 min.**

Share mobiles

9. Examine mobile displays. Read the words and sentences. Observe and discuss various ways classmates achieved balance in their mobiles.

**Assessment**

• Is mobile physically balanced?

| K-2 | 3-4 | 5-6 |
|---|---|---|
| • Is each antonym pair hung from a common branch? | • Is each homonym pair hung from a common branch? | • Do subject, predicate, and direct object all appear on the same level as they would on the baseline of a sentence diagram? |
| • Does bold use of color and imagery make illustrations easy to see from a distance? | • Does bold use of color and imagery make illustrations easy to see from a distance? | • Has student accurately identified subject, predicate, and direct object? |
| • Do illustrations emphasize contrasting characteristics of the antonym pairs? | • Do separate images accurately reflect the individual definition of each homonym? | • Are modifiers accurately suspended from the words they modify? |
| | • Are correct forms of homonyms used in the sample sentences? | • Do all words from the original sentence appear on the mobile? |

• Ask students to reflect on this lesson and write a DREAM statement to summarize the most important things they learned.

**Extensions**

Plan a visit to a local park or art museum where mobiles are on display. Sketch them and record the names of the works and artists. Research information about them to learn more about how mobiles are constructed.

Explore a variety of ways balance plays a role in human lives such as weight scale, balance beam, see-saw, symmetry in design, and human balance regulated by the inner ear.

Encourage students who are learning English as a second language to share examples of antonyms or homonyms from their first language. Ask older students to explain syntactical differences they notice between the two languages. For example, in Spanish, adjectives appear <u>after</u> the nouns they modify. *Casa roja* is literally "house red" rather than "red house" as it would be in English.

Make "Get Acquainted" mobiles by shaping small objects related to personal interests out of Model Magic. Hang mobiles during the first week of school.

Provide a place for younger students and those with special needs to hang their mobiles while they work on them. If possible, provide one-on-one student assistance to avoid frustration during the assembly process.

Challenge students with exceptional spatial and linguistic intelligence to create more complex mobiles by adding more words or word pairs. Fifth and sixth grade students might add prepositional phrases and/or indirect objects to their diagrams.

**Mt. Saint Helens**
**Obsidian Chime Mobile**
2005
Artist unknown
Needles of obsidian,
driftwood, seed pod,
and cord
Pacific Northwest
Private Collection.

**Whale and Fish Mobile**
Artist unknown
Painted wood, string
16" x 24"
Collection of Kevin and
Paula Zelienka.

# Install a Web of Synonymous Words!

## Objectives

Students (K-2) exhibit an understanding of new and challenging synonyms by accurately pairing similar words.

Students (3-6) demonstrate an understanding of precise word choice by explaining variations in synonym meanings.

Students design 3-D installation art for display in a large space.

## Multiple Intelligences

**Linguistic**
**Spatial**

## What Does It Mean?

**Genre:** class or category of artistic endeavor having a particular form, content, or technique

**Installation art:** contemporary art that places the viewer within a specific environment, found both indoors and outdoors, often use familiar objects repeatedly

**Medium:** material or technique with which an artist works

**Thought bubble:** enclosed space in which a character's ideas are portrayed in words or pictures, as in a comic strip

## National Standards

**Visual Arts Standard #2**
Using knowledge of structures and functions

**Visual Arts Standard #6**
Making connections between visual arts and other disciplines

**English Language Arts Standard #3**
Students apply a wide range of strategies to comprehend, interpret, evaluate, and appreciate texts. They draw on their prior experience, their interactions with other readers and writers, their knowledge of word meaning and of other texts, their word identification strategies, and their understanding of textual features (e.g., sound-letter correspondence, sentence structure, context, graphics).

**English Language Arts Standard #9**
Students develop an understanding of and respect for diversity in language use, patterns and dialects across cultures, ethnic groups, geographic regions, and social roles.

## Background Information

The genre of installation art may seem realistic, humorous, chaotic, or even nonsensical. There is no limit to the imagination artists can put into creating installation art. Works of this genre are vastly different in their presentation as well as in the moods and thoughts that they evoke. One especially unique type of this art form is to sculpt a space using several familiar or unusual materials, rather than sculpting an object using one medium.

## Resources

*Charlotte's Web* by E.B. White
When the words "Some Pig!" mysteriously appear in a web over the head of Wilbur, the pig, a miracle is declared and his life is saved. Classic story that appeals to all elementary students. A natural impetus for a word web vocabulary activity.

*Installation Art in the New Millennium:*
*The Empire of the Senses* by Nicholas De Oliveira, Nicola Oxley, and Michael Petry
Introduces teachers to an exciting art form that creates multi-sensory environments. Invites viewers to enter the art work and participate. Inspiration for many classroom uses.

*The American Heritage Children's Thesaurus*
by Paul Hellweg
For grades 3 to 6. Color coding and photo illustrations make this version attractive and easy to use. Lists synonyms and similar words as well as parts of speech.

*The Very Busy Spider* by Eric Carle
Excellent springboard for a discussion of spider webs. Tactile illustrations are especially appealing to children who benefit from kinesthetic learning experiences.

## Vocabulary List

*Use this list to explore new vocabulary,*
*create idea webs, or brainstorm related subjects.*

- Art vocabulary

| | | |
|---|---|---|
| Balance | Emphasis | Outline |
| Complementary colors | Environment | Segment |
| Contrast | Horizontal | Thought bubble |
| Diameter | Installation | |

- Synonym pairs for primary grades

| | | |
|---|---|---|
| Big/large | Make/create | Two/double |
| Friend/buddy | One/single | Wish/hope |
| Go/leave | Pretty/cute | Yellow/gold |
| Little/tiny | Say/tell | |

- Vocabulary from *Charlotte's Web*
  Captivity
  Determined
  Enchanted
  Glutton
  Gullible
  Injustice
  Loathe
  Neglect
  Patient
  Radiant
  Salutations
  Vanished

**Native American Dream-Catcher**
Artist unknown
Willow, feathers, nylon, stone
6" x 6"
Private Collection.

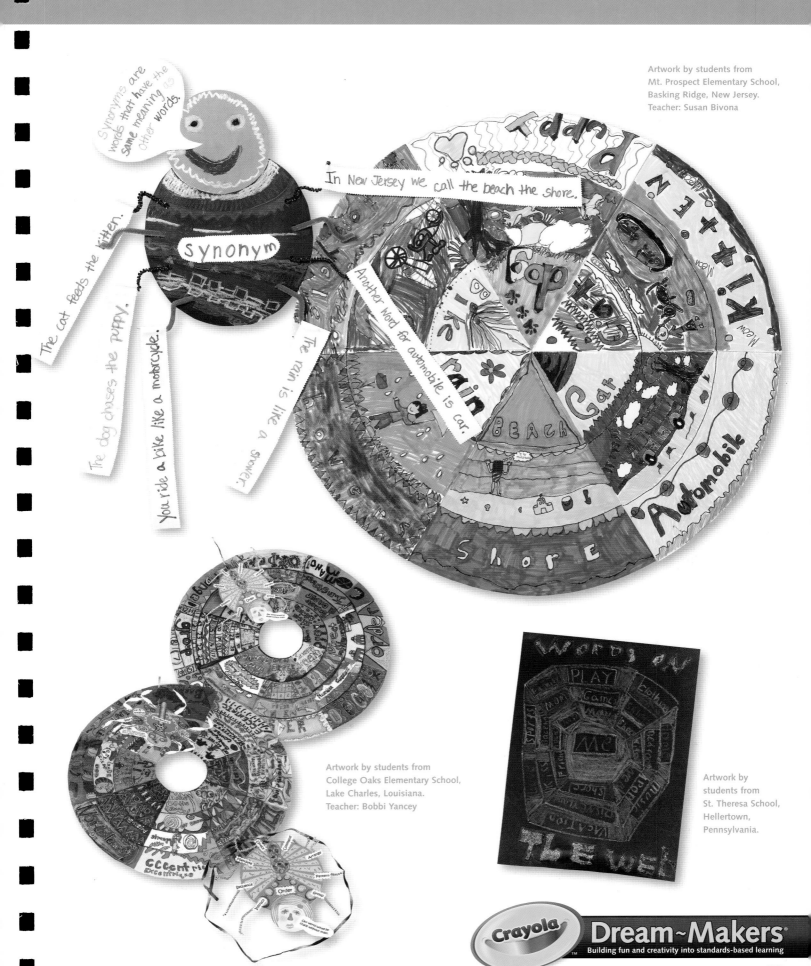

Crayola

Dream~Makers®
Building fun and creativity into standards-based learning

# Install a Web of Synonymous Words!

| | K-2 | 3-4 | 5-6 |
|---|---|---|---|
| **Suggested Preparation and Discussion** | Choose several age-appropriate children's dictionaries and thesauruses. Together, read books that are about spiders and/or contain lots of words for which synonyms can be identified. Display books about spiders. | Read and discuss *The Very Busy Spider* or another spider story. Pose this riddle: "Elizabeth, Betty, Betsy, and Bess went out to the woods to see a bird's nest. How many went?" Although it appears to be four, the answer is one because all four names refer to the same person. With children, create a bulletin board about nicknames. | Assign *Charlotte's Web* or other fiction or non-fiction about spiders. Create a class banner titled Synonyms. Jot down challenging new words from readings. Divide into small groups of six or eight students. Each group selects one word and finds as many synonyms as possible. Discuss nuances of meanings for each. |
| | Explain the concepts of word webs and synonyms. List word pairs, including both familiar and challenging vocabulary words, found in assigned readings. Research installation art. Display reproductions of installation art such as work by Sandy Skoglund on a bulletin board. Discuss Skoglund's art and the question "What is installation art?" | | |
| **Crayola® Supplies** | • Construction Paper™ Crayons  • Markers  • Oil Pastels  • Scissors | | |
| | • Glue Sticks | | • Glitter Glue |
| **Other Materials** | • Construction paper  • Recycled newspaper  • Rulers  • White craft paper  • White paper | | |
| | • Chenille stems  • Clear adhesive tape  • Hole punch  • String or yarn | | |
| **Set-up/Tips** | • Invite parent or student volunteers to cut large craft paper circles. Make circles as big as possible. Divide and cut circles into four sections. Create enough circles so each student has one section. | | |
| | • Demonstrate how to emphasize words and designs by contrasting lights and darks, using complementary colors, and outlining areas. | | |
| **Process: Session 1 20-30 min.** | **Identify synonyms** 1. Students think of other words for *friend*. List responses. 2. Think of other synonymous word pairs. Include familiar and challenging vocabulary from readings. | **List synonymous words** 1. Students research the definition of *synonym*. Select several examples of synonymous words. 2. Discuss the accuracy of the examples. Use a thesaurus. | **Identify "About Me" words** 1. Students list colorful, descriptive words about themselves, such as hobbies, family, friends, movies, sports, and things they enjoy. |
| **Process: Session 2 45-50 min.** | **Create team webs** 3. Children lay circle segments flat so tips point away from them. Divide segments into three horizontal sections separated by lines. | | **Create personal webs** 2. Draw a large circle on construction paper. 3. Divide the circle into segments that radiate from a center point similar to a spider web. Make four or five sections. 4. Write headline words from the About Me list around the perimeter. 5. Fill each segment with synonymous words aligned to the headline word. |
| | 4. Each child selects a pair of synonyms from the list. Write one word in the lower third of the section and the other word in the upper third. Leave the middle section blank. 5. Illustrate the synonyms' meaning in the middle section. | 4. Divide into groups of four. Each group chooses one word and looks for synonyms in a thesaurus. 5. Students write four or five synonyms in their segments. | 6. Title the web, such as All About Me. 7. Embellish the title with glitter glue. Air-dry the glue. |

| | K-2 | 3-4 | 5-6 |
|---|---|---|---|
| **Process: Session 3 45-50 min.** | **Make spiders** <br><br> 6. In small groups or individually, cut 9-inch diameter circles from construction paper to make spider bodies. Cut 4-inch circles for heads. Glue circles so the head overlaps the body. <br><br> 7. Punch a hole in the spider's body for hanging. <br><br> 8. Cut four chenille stems in half for legs. Bend. Tape legs to the back of the spider's body, four on each side. Decorate the spider's body and facial features. | | **Make a web wall** <br><br> 8. Create a banner with a title such as "All About Me Web Installation" <br><br> 9. Hang it on a wall above the web designs. |
| | | 9. Cut strips of white paper. Write sentences using *synonym* pairs on the strips. Glue strips to the spider legs. <br><br> 10. Write the word synonym on another strip. Glue it to the spider body. <br><br> 11. Cut a paper thought bubble. Define the word *synonym* on the bubble. Glue it to the spider head. | |
| | Hang spiders with webs made of string. | | |
| **Assessment** | • Are word pairs synonymous and spelled correctly? Are sentences accurate? <br><br> • Do words stand out against the background? Is the art rich and inviting? <br><br> • Are spiders constructed according to directions and with parts labeled properly? <br><br> • Is the work effective as a large installation piece? | • Do webs have multiple synonyms for the same word? Can students explain the similarities and differences between the definitions of the synonyms? <br><br> • Are spiders and webs artistically and physically balanced, making them good examples of installation art? | • Do individual webs have headline words in the perimeter? <br><br> • Do the words within each section relate to the headline word? <br><br> • How well do the descriptive words reflect the student who created the web? <br><br> • Ask students to look at webs and match webs to individuals in class. |
| | • Ask students to reflect on this lesson and write a DREAM statement to summarize the most important things they learned. | | |
| **Extensions** | Invite students to design installation art for a local playground or other large facility. Discuss results. Present most practical ideas to local officials and request an opportunity to plan a community service activity focused on this project. <br><br> Suggest that students write creative stories, leaving blanks to fill in with one of several synonyms. Exchange stories so classmates finish each other's stories. <br><br> Encourage students who enjoy word play to create a mix-and-match synonyms game with words and pictures. Provide time for entire class to play. | | |
| | Plan a field trip for younger students and those with kinesthetic needs to the site of an installation art project. | | Challenge academically talented students to trace the origin of the word *synonym* and other words with similar roots. Ask them to share their findings with the class. |

**Crocheted Doily**
Artist unknown
Cotton thread
6" x 6"
Private Collection.

Crayola Dream~Makers®
Building fun and creativity into standards-based learning

# Words on the Brain Game

## Objectives

Students use various sculpting techniques to create busts that include visible "brain matter."

Students create word games using language appropriate to their ages and ability levels. Students use words that come from assigned readings of fiction or non-fiction literature.

Students correlate signs and symbols with words. Older students use words from vocabulary lists related to recent studies in language arts and across content areas, using dictionary definitions.

## Multiple Intelligences

| Interpersonal | Spatial |
|---|---|
| Linguistic | |

## National Standards

| **Visual Arts Standard #5** | **English Language Arts Standard #3** |
|---|---|
| Reflecting upon and assessing the characteristics and merits of their work and the work of others | Students apply a wide range of strategies to comprehend, interpret, evaluate, and appreciate texts. They draw on their prior experience, their interactions with other readers and writers, their knowledge of word meaning and of other texts, their word identification strategies, and their understanding of textual features (e.g., sound-letter correspondence, sentence structure, context, graphics). |

## What Does It Mean?

**Bust:** sculpture representing a person's head, shoulders, and upper chest

**Visible "brain matter":** three-dimensional forms attached to the back of a model head to represent the right and left hemisphere of the brain

## Background Information

Humans' heads are absolutely necessary in order for us to move, see, smell, taste, and hear. They are also the location of our brains. When we hear or see information repeatedly, it begins to stick in our minds. This lesson playfully makes the point that reviewing vocabulary words helps them "stick" in children's minds.

## Resources

*Art Fun (Art and Activities for Kids)* edited by Kim Solga
Appropriate for grades 1 to 6, this book includes a separate section on sculptures.

*How Does Your Brain Work?* by Don L. Curry, Nancy R. Vargus, and Su Tien Wong
The simple text and illustrations teach the various functions of different parts of the brain and make complex information understandable even for young children.

*Scholastic Children's Dictionary* from Scholastic
With easy-to-understand definitions, sample sentences, synonyms, illustrations, and photographs, this is a good dictionary for ages 8 to 12.

## Vocabulary List

*Some of the vocabulary listed below may be helpful, but most important for this lesson is to use vocabulary from recent classroom lessons appropriate to the ages and ability levels of the students.*

- Art vocabulary

| Bust | Proportion |
|---|---|
| Clay | Sculpture |
| Form | Texture |
| Model | |

- Language vocabulary

| Definition | Synonym |
|---|---|
| Dictionary | Thesaurus |

- Brain vocabulary

| Brainstem | Cerebral cortex |
|---|---|
| Cerebellum | Forebrain |
| | Ganglia |
| | Hemisphere |
| | Medulla |
| | Memory |
| | Midbrain |
| | Neurons |
| | Spinal cord |

Artwork by students from St. Theresa School, Hellertown, Pennsylvania.

Artwork by students from
Mt. Prospect Elementary School,
Basking Ridge, New Jersey.
Teacher: Susan Bivona

Words on the Brain

festival    ancestors    heritage    holiday

immigrant

Words on The Brain
Vocabulary words

Symbol

tradition

legend

Ancestors are the people in your family who lived before.

A story that tells about a belief of people.

A festival is a celebration.

A holiday is a day on which people or events are honored.

Something handed down from earlier generations of from the past such as a tradition.

painter

painter' (pànt'ər) n. 1. an artist who paints pictures. 2. a person whose work is covering surfaces, as walls, with paint.

Something that stands for something else.

A building where objects of art, science or history are displayed for people to see.

Artwork by students
from St. Theresa School,
Hellertown, Pennsylvania.

Crayola Dream~Makers®
Building fun and creativity into standards-based learning

Language Arts    79

# Words on the Brain Game

| | K-2 | 3-4 | 5-6 |
|---|---|---|---|
| **Suggested Preparation and Discussion** | Create and display a diagram or model of the human brain. Be prepared to discuss how the brain works. Indicate the section of the brain that is devoted to language acquisition. <br><br> Display several sample sculpture busts in class to use as visual reference. Create an example of a completed "Words on the Brain" game to show students. <br><br> Explain that the objective of the lesson is to increase vocabulary knowledge and usage by creating a vocabulary game with a game box, decorated envelope, word cards, and a modeled head. <br><br> With students, identify vocabulary words from fiction or non-fiction literature assignments. | | |
| **Crayola® Supplies** | • Colored Pencils   • Markers   • Model Magic®   • Paint Brushes   • School Glue   • Scissors   • Tempera Paint | | |
| **Other Materials** | • Colored paper   • Foam balls (approximately 3" in diameter)   • Foil paper   • Oak tag or recycled file folders <br> • Paper clips (large)   • Recycled newspaper   • Recycled, clean plastic containers (such as yogurt or cottage cheese) <br> • Shoeboxes (large)   • Water containers   • White rolled paper   • Wide-mouth plastic jars with lids (optional) <br> • Yarn | | |
| **Set-up/Tips** | • Ask parent volunteers to save and send shoeboxes with lids. <br> • Instead of foam balls, consider using lightly crumpled balls of aluminum foil as armatures for the heads. <br> • As an alternative to envelopes, use a large-mouth juice bottle as a base for individual projects. Store word cards inside the container. <br> • Cover the painting area with newspaper. | | |
| **Process: Session 1 30-45 min.** | **Create word cards** <br> 1. Students review new words from assigned readings. Encourage them to choose nouns or other words that can be easily represented with symbols. <br> 2. Cut oak tag into word cards. Write one word on one side of the card. Add borders or other decorative elements to enrich the card. <br> 3. Draw a symbol on the back of each card representing the word written on the front. | **Create word cards** <br> 1. Teams of students make lists of new vocabulary words they identify from fiction or non-fiction literature assignments. <br> 2. Cut oak tag into unusually shaped word cards. Decorate the edges of the cards. Write one vocabulary word on one side of each card and the word's definition on the back. <br> 3. Exchange cards to check for correct word meanings. | **Creating topic-specific word cards** <br> 1. Pairs or small groups of students identify and research topic-specific vocabulary from assigned readings. <br> 2. List words from content areas such as science or math. <br> 3. Cut oak tag into unusually shaped word cards. Write one word on the front of each card and the correct dictionary definition on the back. Decorate cards. |
| | **Create a word bank** <br> 4. Students make a title label to attach to the side of a wide-mouth plastic jar. | **Create a word bank** <br> 4. Teams of students cover a shoebox with white paper and decorate it. Write the title of the game in bold lettering on the lid. | |
| **Process: Session 2 20-30 min.** | **Sculpt the heads** <br> 5. Loosely cover a foam ball with small, flat Model Magic pieces. Sculpt realistic eyes, nose, ears, and mouth on the face. Model the back of the head to look like 3-D brain matter. <br> 6. Cover an upside-down plastic container with Model Magic coils. Use this as a base or neck on which to set the head form. <br> 7. Insert glue-covered ends of eight large paper clips into the top and back of the head. Air-dry at least 24 hours. | | |

| | K-2 | 3-4 | 5-6 |
|---|---|---|---|
| **Process:**<br>**Session 3**<br>**30-45 min.** | **Decorate the heads**<br>**8.** Paint the sculpted heads. Air-dry the paint<br>**9.** Cut and glue yarn to the head to simulate hair. Air-dry the glue. | | |
| **Process:**<br>**Session 4**<br>**30-45 min.** | **Store learned words**<br>**10.** Place the newly learned words in word banks for storage and easy reference. Attach them to heads for display. | **Build vocabulary**<br>**10.** Challenge the students to discuss possible ways to turn vocabulary building into a game.<br>**11.** Decide on directions agreeable to all. Post them. Students play their own games first and then exchange games with others until all have had a chance to play several games.<br>**12.** Discuss similarities and differences in the games. | |
| **Assessment** | • Do sculpted heads have realistic, human characteristics? Are features proportionate to the head size? Does the brain clearly show two hemispheres? Is texturing realistic?<br>• Are vocabulary words spelled correctly?<br>• Ask students to reflect on this lesson and write a DREAM statement to summarize the most important things they learned. | | |
| | • Do symbols on the backs of the cards clearly represent the words on the front? | • Do definitions on the backs of the cards clearly define the words on the front?<br>• Is the box clearly labeled with the name of the game? Are designs colorful and inviting? Do all parts of game fit in box? | |
| **Extensions** | Visit a local sculpture garden or museum.<br>Consider identifying themes for vocabulary-building games.<br>Invite a nurse, physician, or scientist to talk about how the brain works.<br>Students with special needs may use a computer to create text and illustrations for the word cards.<br>Cover the sculpture with Crayola Pearl It! Tempera Mixing Medium to give it an interesting sheen. | | |
| | | Invite students who are gifted with strong language arts skills to use a thesaurus to find challenging new synonyms for familiar words. | |

**Massai Tribal Member Bust**
2005
Artist: Ben Apollo
Modeled clay
4" x 4 1/2" x 8"
Kenya
Private Collection.

**Burmese Puppet Head**
Circa 1900s
Artist unknown
Carved and painted wood, wire, animal hair
4" x 4 1/2" x 8"
Burma
Private Collection.

Crayola **Dream~Makers®**
Building fun and creativity into standards-based learning

# Mix-and-Match Vocabulary Books

## Objectives

Students identify definitions and visual symbols for new words to expand their comprehension of vocabulary.

Primary students design two-part mix-and-match vocabulary books using their writing, spelling, decoding, and drawing skills.

Students (3-6) create three-part mix-and-match vocabulary books as an aid to learning definitions of and visual symbols for new words.

## Multiple Intelligences

Bodily-kinesthetic
Linguistic
Spatial

## What Does It Mean?

**Visual symbols:** commonly understood representations of ideas, such a heart meaning love

**Visualize:** process of recalling or imagining mental pictures

## National Standards

**Visual Arts Standard #3**
Choosing and evaluating a range of subject matter, symbols, and ideas

**Visual Arts Standard #5**
Reflecting upon and assessing the characteristics and merits of their work and the work of others

**English Language Arts Standard #3**
Students apply a wide range of strategies to comprehend, interpret, evaluate, and appreciate texts. They draw on their prior experience, their interactions with other readers and writers, their knowledge of word meaning and of other texts, their word identification strategies, and their understanding of textual features (e.g., sound-letter correspondence, sentence structure, context, graphics).

**English Language Arts Standard #10**
Students whose first language is not English make use of their first language to develop competency in the English language arts and to develop understanding of content across the curriculum.

## Background Information

Children enjoy mix-and-match books that combine animals' or peoples' heads, bodies, and feet. This format enables them to match related bits of information. The more accustomed children are to matching words, definitions, and illustrations, the more fluent they are likely to be in understanding vocabulary words. The physical act of drawing visual symbols to represent words and flipping through the parts of a mix-and-match book both reinforce vocabulary study through kinesthetic learning.

## Resources

*Best Picture Dictionary Ever!* illustrated by Richard Scarry
Delightful animal characters depict more than 700 words. Sentences demonstrate various uses for each word. Related words such as *airplane, jet, control tower,* and *stewardess* are introduced in detailed scenes. Ages 4 to 8.

*Dancing With Words: Helping Students Love Language Through Authentic Vocabulary Instruction* by Judith Rowe Michaels
A sensory approach to the study of vocabulary. Encourages students and teachers to bring life experiences to discussions of language. Also explores voice and connotation. National Council of Teachers of English publication for middle school and older.

*Scranimals* by Jack Prelutsky
Zany poetry about mixed-up animals such as Broccolions and Spinachickens that live on Scranimal Island. Readers' creative juices flow.

*The Mix and Match Book of Bugs* by Sally Rose
Designed for 4- to 8-year-olds. Colorful example of a mix-and-match flip book inspires all students making such books.

## Vocabulary List

*Create vocabulary lists directly related to classroom studies. For new readers, write lists of words students are learning to recognize in their reading. For older students, draw on vocabulary from literature studies or from the science or social studies curriculum. This is also an excellent technique for learning a second language.*

| | |
|---|---|
| Bind | Shape |
| Context | Texture |
| Define | Unity |
| Definition | Visualize |

Artwork by students from
Holly Glen Elementary
School, Williamstown,
New Jersey.
Teacher: Patricia Skalka

Mix and Match Vocabulary Book

Turnip
An orangish-brown
vegetable that grows
underground.

Broadcast
Something you watch
on tv that gives you
information.

Garden
A place where flowers, vegetables, and
shrubs are grown

KRAYOLA

A Girl of A Different Color

There was a girl named
Lucy. She had a bad case of
"terdontyosis" which means that
every thing on your body turns
different colors. She loved it. So
she went to the library to
check out this disease. When
she was there, she started to feel.
Lucy looked down but her bangs
were in her face. She lifted up her
hair and saw that her lower body
turned into a chin. For her, it was
not that bad she just decided to
keep her chin up

The End

Artwork by students from
Mt. Prospect Elementary School,
Basking Ridge, New Jersey.
Teacher: Regina De Francisco

Crayola Dream~Makers®
Building fun and creativity into standards-based learning

# Mix-and-Match Vocabulary Books

| | K-2 | 3-4 | 5-6 |
|---|---|---|---|
| **Suggested Preparation and Discussion** | Display examples of mix-and-match books as well as other vocabulary-building resources such as children's dictionaries. Include one or two original examples that follow the project guidelines. | | |
| | With students, create and post a list of sight words they are learning. Select only words that can be easily illustrated such as concrete nouns.<br><br>Students take turns reading the words aloud. Discuss what they picture (visualize) in their minds when they read these words. | With students, create and post a list of vocabulary words related to a current unit of study or ask students to make lists of their own from books they are reading. Remind students that concrete nouns will be easiest to illustrate, but encourage those who are willing to accept the challenge to explore other possibilities as well.<br><br>Students take turns defining words based on what they have been learning or on the context in which the words were used. Check definitions in a dictionary. | |
| **Crayola® Supplies** | • Erasable Colored Pencils   • Markers   • Scissors | | |
| **Other Materials** | • Hole punch   • Index cards (4- x 6-inch, lined on one side)   • Oak tag   • Yarn, ribbon, or metal rings | | |

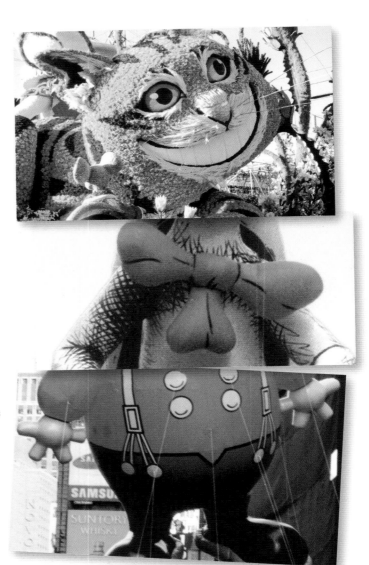

Macy's Day Parade Balloon Images
New York, New York
Photograph: R. De Long

| | K-2 | 3-4 | 5-6 |
|---|---|---|---|

**Process: Session 1 20-30 min.**

**Make word cards**

1. Ask each student to choose a different word from the vocabulary list.

2. On the lined side of an index card, write the assigned word. Pay attention to letter formation and accurate spelling.

3. Outline the word shape with bold, colorful markers. (Associating shape with words is an aid to decoding.)

4. On the unlined side of a second card, draw a picture that shows what students see in their minds when they read the word. Draw large, bold images.

**Prepare detailed word cards**

1. Children choose one unique word from the vocabulary list.

2. On the unlined side of an index card, write the chosen word, spelled correctly, using bold colors and lettering.

3. On a second card, define the word as it is used in context of readings. Again, attend to the spelling.

4. On a third card, illustrate the word's meaning. Personalize illustrations. For example, an *edifice* is a building. Rather than drawing a typical rectangular skyscraper, draw a specific building such as the school, a local store, or a favorite museum. Textured details (brick, stone, concrete) add interest and definition to the visualization.

**Process: Session 2 15-20 min.**

**Match words and illustrations**

5. Divide into small groups at a table or in a circle on the floor. Collect and shuffle the cards. Lay out cards in the center so everyone can see them. Take turns matching words and pictures. Exchange groups of cards and repeat until all sets have been matched by all groups.

**Process: Session 3 10-15 min.**

**Create vocabulary books**

6. Create small group vocabulary books by punching holes in the left side of the cards. Use ribbon, yarn, or metal rings to bind them together.

7. Ask student volunteers to cut a cover with oak tag or recycled file folders. Decorate the cover to create a unified presentation.

**Assessment**

- Are words spelled correctly? Was color used to boldly outline them?
- Do drawings visually symbolize and accurately represent the intended words?
- Can students match classmates' words and pictures as well as their own?
- Ask students to reflect on this lesson and write a DREAM statement to summarize the most important things they learned.

**Extensions**

Keep the books handy for students to review their vocabulary and spelling skills. Encourage children to make their own books, especially for words that they find challenging.

Use the word cards for a game. Form two teams. One member of each team sees the same word card and draws visual clues so their teammates can identify and spell the word.

As a fun follow-up activity, share Jack Prelutsky's *Behold the Bold Umbrellaphant* or *Scranimals*. With these books students will soon delight in the pure joy of word play. Advanced students might try writing some of their own "mixed up word" poems.

Children learning a second language can use the books and related game to build their vocabularies.

Crayola **Dream~Makers**
Building fun and creativity into standards-based learning

# Celebrate Diversity With Multicultural Banners

## Objectives

Students read literature with multicultural themes and explore vocabulary and concepts associated with the values of appreciating diversity.

Students make banners using positive symbols that reflect and synthesize their knowledge about multicultural diversity on either a personal, national, or international level.

## Multiple Intelligences

Interpersonal
Intrapersonal
Linguistic

## What Does It Mean?

**Indigenous:** native; originating in and characteristic of a particular region or country

**Positive symbols:** favorable representations of an idea or object

## National Standards

| Visual Arts Standard #4 Understanding the visual arts in relation to history and cultures | **English Language Arts Standard #1** Students read a wide range of print and nonprint texts to build an understanding of texts, of themselves, and of the cultures of the United States and the world; to acquire new information; to respond to the needs and demands of society and the workplace; and for personal fulfillment. Among these texts are fiction and nonfiction, classic and contemporary works. *Grades K-2* **English Language Arts Standard #3** Students apply a wide range of strategies to comprehend, interpret, evaluate, and appreciate texts. They draw on their prior experience, their interactions with other readers and writers, their knowledge of word meaning and of other texts, their word identification strategies, and their understanding of textual features (e.g., sound-letter correspondence, sentence structure, context, graphics). *Grades 5-6* **English Language Arts Standard #8** Students use a variety of technological and information resources (e.g., libraries, databases, computer networks, video) to gather and synthesize information and to create and communicate knowledge. **English Language Arts Standard #12** Students use spoken, written, and visual language to accomplish their own purposes (e.g., for learning, enjoyment, persuasion, and the exchange of information). |
|---|---|

## Background Information

The United States of America has often been referred to as "a nation of immigrants." It is a country with a widely diverse population, which makes it unique in the world.

In 1963 the Rev. Dr. Martin Luther King, Jr., described his multicultural dream for America. King stated, "I have a dream that one day on the red hills of Georgia, the sons of former slaves and the sons of former slave owners will be able to sit down together at the table of brotherhood... I have a dream that with this faith we will be able to transform the jangling discords of our nation into a beautiful symphony of brotherhood."

People who attend rallies often carry signs and banners that tell others about their thoughts and beliefs on a topic or idea. Banners have been used, like flags, as a means of unifying people. They have been used to advocate for a cause and applaud accomplishments. Multicultural banners celebrate diversity and unify those who might otherwise see themselves as being different.

## Resources

*All the Colors of the Earth* by Sheila Hamanaka
Beautiful introduction to the celebration of diversity. Poetic text and eloquent art celebrate Earth and its peoples.

*Chicken Sunday* by Patricia Polacco
A young Polish American girl and her two African American neighbors befriend an elderly Jewish shopkeeper when he is harassed by some older boys. Depicts a multicultural neighborhood and celebrates its diversity.

*In the Year of the Boar and Jackie Robinson*
by Bette Bao Lord
Nine-year-old Shirley Temple Wong arrives in Brooklyn in 1947, the year Jackie Robinson breaks the color barrier in baseball. Deals with issues of immigration, race, and acceptance on an elementary level. Includes a humorous chapter about learning the Pledge of Allegiance.

*www.teachingtolerance.org*
The Southern Poverty Law Center is devoted to issues of tolerance and acceptance. Publishes outstanding, free materials for teachers including award-winning videos and a magazine of ideas for multicultural education.

## Vocabulary List

*Use this list to explore new vocabulary, create idea webs, or brainstorm related subjects.*

| | | |
|---|---|---|
| Acceptance | Harmony | Religion |
| Appreciation | Ideals | Rights |
| Balance | Identity | Sharing |
| Banners | Immigrant/immigration | Similarities |
| Bias | Indigenous | Stereotypes |
| Bilingual | Justice | Symbols |
| Celebrations | Languages | Texture |
| Commonalities | Migration | Togetherness |
| Community | Motto | Tolerance |
| Culture | Multilingual | Unique |
| Differences | Peace | Unity |
| Diversity | Portraits | Values |
| Equality | Prejudice | |
| Ethnic | Race | |

Artwork by students from
Hillar Elementary School,
Madison Heights, Michigan.
Teachers: Craig Hinshaw and
Therese Sadlier

Artwork by student from
Chicago Public Schools.

Banners can be represented by flags. Many
cultures include flags in ceremonies. Flags and
banner drapery often include colors that hold
specific meaning.

# Celebrate Diversity With Multicultural Banners

| | K-2 | 3-4 | 5-6 |
|---|---|---|---|
| **Suggested Preparation and Discussion** | Display portraits reflecting diversity of race, age, and other human characteristics. Hang sample banners, including one done with the assignment techniques and theme. Together, read a book with a multicultural theme that is meaningful to the students and will spark relevant discussion. | | |
| | **Focus: Our Multicultural Community**<br><br>Introduce the terms *similarities* and *differences*.<br><br>Ask students to think of ways they are similar to and different from people they know. Consider unique characteristics (names, birthdates, favorite colors) and cultural heritage (customs, foods, holidays) as well as physical features.<br><br>Explain to students that they will make a banner showing how they and their classmates have both similarities and differences. Explain another word for *different* is *unique*. | **Focus: Our Multicultural Country**<br><br>Introduce the phrase *cultural diversity*. Examine the history of diversity in the United States from indigenous peoples to current immigrants. How have various cultures added to the richness of the country?<br><br>Explain to children that they will create a banner highlighting the beauty and contributions of individuals from diverse cultures who live in the United States. | **Focus: Our Multicultural World**<br><br>Discuss the word *stereotype*. What does it mean? How does stereotyping contribute to misunderstandings among people? How can it be overcome?<br><br>Identify other vocabulary words related to the study of world cultures and languages. Why is it important for people to understand and value other cultures?<br><br>Tell students they will create a banner with positive symbols representing appreciation for the similarities and differences of people from various world cultures. |
| **Crayola® Supplies** | • Multicultural Markers   • School Glue   • Scissors   • Slick Stix™ Crayons | | |
| **Other Materials** | • Craft paper on a roll (colored and white) | | |
| | • Index cards   • Overhead projector<br>• Yarn or string | • Construction paper   • Map of United States | |
| **Process: Session 1**<br><br>Grades K-2<br>20-30 min.<br><br>Grades 3-4<br>45-60 min.<br><br>Grades 5-6<br>Several 45-min. sessions | **Create self-portraits**<br>1. Attach white craft paper to a wall. Assist children to use an overhead projector to work in teams to outline each other on the paper.<br>2. Color the outlines and add details with multicultural markers and Slick Stix. Cut out the figures. | **Research diversity within the United States**<br>1. Research and discuss cultural groups in the United States. Use children's own heritages and people within the community to illustrate indigenous peoples and immigrants, both historic and current.<br>2. Brainstorm ways to represent these groups symbolically and in an affirming manner. Consider realistic portraits of people as well as traditional clothing, crafts, food, music, languages, and other cultural characteristics. | **Research and create international cultural images**<br>1. Students form small groups and select a culture to research. Encourage them to use Web sites and books to identify images representative of the chosen culture.<br>2. Using multicultural markers and Slick Stix, students create colorful cultural images and symbols inspired by the research. |
| **Process: Session 2**<br>30-45 min. | **Add words to define self**<br>3. Cut at least three index cards in half. Children write one personal characteristic about themselves on each half.<br>4. Decorate cards with unifying borders and designs. Glue to figures. Air-dry the glue. | **Create visual images**<br>3. On construction paper, create at least six symbols reflecting the cultural diversity of the United States using multicultural markers and Slick Stix.<br>4. Color the images and cut them out. | **Share ideas and design banner**<br>3. Students share results of their research with the class. Discuss similarities and differences among cultures. What stereotypes proved to be untrue based on their research?<br>4. As a group, select a message to communicate with a multicultural banner. Discuss design ideas. Consider ways of combining visual images and words to communicate the message. |

| | K-2 | 3-4 | 5-6 |
|---|---|---|---|
| **Process: Session 3 30-45 min.** | **Design banner** <br> 5. Cut craft paper for banner background. <br> 6. Discuss characteristics that unite the class. Select one. Agree on a symbolic image of that idea (such as a class photo or motto). Place it in the center of the banner. Glue figures around the central image. <br> 7. Children look for commonalities among themselves. Use yarn to connect the similarities. Children find at least three connections with others in the class. Discuss similarities and differences. | **Design banner** <br> 5. Cut a large outline map of the United States on colored craft paper. Glue it to the center of much larger white craft paper base. Glue images across the map in a way that looks balanced and unified. <br> 6. Together, list words related to cultural diversity. Discuss possible messages to convey. Agree on a title. Write it on the banner in bubble letters. Add texture by filling letters with patterns and designs. <br> 7. Add colorful, positive words and images related to cultural diversity to the banner. | **Create banner** <br> 5. On craft paper, prepare the background and work on different areas of the banner to carry out the design idea to express unity through diversity. |
| **Process: Session 4 20-30 min.** | 8. Agree on a banner title. Write it in large, embellished letters above the banner. Add designs and patterns for a balanced presentation. | | |
| | 9. Together, hang the banner in a prominent place. | | |
| **Assessment** | • Are children's six (or more) defining personal characteristics descriptive, legibly written, and correctly spelled? <br> • Do yarn connections accurately reflect similarities? <br> • Do banner images work together to reflect a spirit of unity? <br> • Do children's oral statements about themselves and others reflect an appreciation for their differences as well as their similarities? | • Children create at least six affirming symbols of cultural diversity. <br> • Are vocabulary words legibly written and correctly spelled? <br> • Do written messages reflect sensitivity to multicultural issues? <br> • Do images reflect in-depth research? <br> • Does the banner carry an important or persuasive message enhanced by color, design, and imagery? | • How clearly can students define and explain the problems of stereotyping? <br> • Is the banner free of stereotypical images and words? <br> • Does the banner design integrate words and well-researched imagery to create a sense of unity? <br> • Did individuals work together harmoniously to produce one banner? |
| | • Ask students to reflect on this lesson and write a DREAM statement to summarize the most important things they learned. | | |
| **Extensions** | Post words children are most likely to need help to spell. Provide computers or adult volunteers to assist children with special needs. <br> Hold a multicultural celebration. Invite children to bring foods representative of their own cultural heritages. Invite community members to demonstrate and/or teach crafts from various cultures. <br> Invite high school exchange students to speak about their native cultures. <br> Encourage children to interview relatives to learn more about their own cultural heritages. | | |
| | | Challenge gifted students to write short stories or articles based on their cultural heritages. <br> Study and debate current issues such as immigration, languages, housing, and human rights. | |

Adinkra and Kente Cloth Designs
Artist: Sandy Eckert
Crayola fabric markers, cloth
12" x 18"
Private Collection.

# Wanted: Colorful Characters!

## Objectives

Students write character sketches using colorful words that describe specific personality traits.

Students draw pictures of attributes that are reflected in personalities.

Students create an illustrated "wanted" poster with text based on character sketches.

## Multiple Intelligences

Interpersonal

Linguistic

## What Does It Mean?

**Character sketch:** brief, descriptive writing or artwork that conveys an individual's traits

**Personality traits:** distinguishing features of one's character

## National Standards

**Visual Arts Standard #3**
Choosing and evaluating a range of subject matter, symbols, and ideas

**Visual Arts Standard #6**
Making connections between visual arts and other disciplines

**English Language Arts Standard #3**
Students apply a wide range of strategies to comprehend, interpret, evaluate, and appreciate texts. They draw on their prior experience, their interactions with other readers and writers, their knowledge of word meaning and of other texts, their word identification strategies, and their understanding of textual features (e.g., sound-letter correspondence, sentence structure, context, graphics).

## Background Information

By the 15th century, posters were used as a means to communicate news and information and slowly began to replace town criers. With the invention of lithography in the 19th century, poster art gained popularity. In France, Jules Cheret, called the Father of the Modern Poster, began to mass produce lithograph posters in color. He combined poster text with imagery to spark curiosity and add interest in advertisements. Today, posters are still used to communicate powerful messages.

## Resources

*A Book About Design: Complicated Doesn't Make It Good* by Mark Gonyea
Written for children. Emphasis is on simplicity of design and the effective use of shape, line, and color. Excellent resource for teaching poster design in elementary schools.

*Because of Winn-Dixie* by Kate DiCamillo
An award winning novel. Excellent example of characterization for older elementary readers.

*http://www.readwritethink.org*
Web site developed through a partnership between the International Reading Association and the National Council of Teachers of English. Goldmine of resources for language arts teachers. Lessons on creating character trading cards and focusing on characterization in novels by Patricia Polacco are particularly good resources for teaching vocabulary related to character traits.

*Saving Sweetness* by Diane Stanley
Lively story set in the old West contrasts a bumbling but good-hearted sheriff with a feisty, quick-witted orphan girl. Both story and illustrations are excellent examples of characterization for young elementary students.

## Vocabulary List

*Sample adjectives used to describe character traits. Use these examples to help students create lists of their own. Encourage older students to use a thesaurus to stretch their vocabularies.*

- Kindergarten-Grade 2

| | |
|---|---|
| Cranky | Selfish |
| Friendly | Sharing |
| Happy | Shy |
| Neat | Strong |

- Grades 3-4

| | |
|---|---|
| Generous | Stingy |
| Lively | Sturdy |
| Orderly | Timid |
| Outgoing | Unpleasant |

- Grades 5-6

| | |
|---|---|
| Beneficent | Meticulous |
| Cantankerous | Possessive |
| Gregarious | Stalwart |
| Introverted | Vivacious |

- Visual arts vocabulary

| | |
|---|---|
| Balance | Repetition |
| Border | Rhythm |
| Emphasis | Shape |
| Pattern | Unity |
| Proportion | Variety |

People who are looking for good homes for their pets often post notices in offices and public bulletin boards.

Artwork by students from
Mt. Prospect Elementary School,
Basking Ridge, New Jersey.
Teacher: Susan Bivona

BE ON THE Lookout For

# MALEFICENT

SHE CAST A SPELL ON SLEEPING BEAUTY

LOOK FOR

Horns on Her Head.
Her body is green.
She wears a black cape.
She carries a Raven.
When she appears, she
appears in a fire.

## WANTED

**Name:** Count Olaf
**Also Known As:** N/A
**Setting:** A house in the city

**Distinguishing Characteristics:**
Unshaven, one eyebrow,
shiny eyes, gray hair,
wheezy voice,
tattoo of an eye on his left
ankle,
he is obsessed with eyes

**Remarks:** Count Olaf is an out of work
actor. He has a **wheezy** voice, it
whistles and squeaks when he talks.
Olaf is **obsessed** with eyes; his house
is full of pictures of them.
He is **cantankerous**; he is always in a
bad mood. He is wanted for trying to
kill the Baudelaire children in
exchange for their family fortune.

## HAVE YOU SEEN...

**Name:** Portia Blake
**Also Known As:** N/A
**Setting:** Camp Gone-Away Lake
**Description:** loyal, adventurous, bold,
fun, cool, positive

**Remarks:** Portia is **loyal**; she stuck up
for her friend when the other kids
made fun of her name. Every summer
she tried to do something new and
exciting. She was very **adventurous**.
Portia is **bold** because she wasn't
afraid to find out what was in Gone-
Away Lake. Portia is a very **positive**
person; she's always happy and makes
other people feel that way.

Artwork by students from
Community School 102,
Bronx, New York.
Teacher: Neila P. Steiner

Crayola **Dream~Makers**
Building fun and creativity into standards-based learning

# Wanted: Colorful Characters!

| | K-2 | 3-4 | 5-6 |
|---|---|---|---|
| **Suggested Preparation and Discussion** | Display a variety of posters with strong visual appeal. Ask children to point out their favorite posters and tell why they like them. Discuss the attributes of good poster design in terms of imagery; use of bold, contrasting colors; and ways in which text and symbols work together for a unified look. What are different kinds of posters? How and where are they used?<br><br>Brainstorm features of personalities to develop character profiles. Read books, magazines, newspapers, and other resources that have well-defined, strong, and interesting characters.<br><br>Make an example of a character trait word list that describes character traits. Differentiate between outward appearance and inner character. | | |
| | Focus on words that are already in children's speaking vocabularies and in challenging reading. Discuss why they are descriptive character words. | Stretch vocabularies by looking up common adjectives in a thesaurus or dictionary to find alternatives that may be more precise. (See the vocabulary section for examples.) | |
| **Crayola® Supplies** | • Colored Pencils  • Glue Sticks  • Markers  • Paint Brushes  • Watercolors | | |
| **Other Materials** | • Poster board  • Recycled newspaper  • Water containers  • White paper | | |
| **Set-up/Tips** | • Cover painting surface with newspaper.<br>• Young students may have more success with fine-point markers rather than watercolors due to the detail involved. | | |
| **Process Session 1 15-20 min.** | **Establish family member profiles**<br><br>1. Make a list of ideal attributes for family members. What are great dads and moms like? How would the best brothers and sisters act? | **Establish a book character profile**<br><br>1. Students select a fictional character.<br><br>2. Create a list of attributes that define the character. | **Establish a world leader profile**<br><br>1. Research current world leaders.<br><br>2. List leaders' positive character attributes.<br><br>3. Forecast what character attributes might be important when they are old enough to vote. Why? |

*Who's On My Bridge?*
*Character Puppets*
Artist: Sandy Eckert
Model Magic®, marker,
watercolor, string, wood
8" x 18"
Private Collection.

| | K-2 | 3-4 | 5-6 |
|---|---|---|---|

**Process:**
**Session 2**
**30-45 min.**

### Illustrate a character

4. Choose a colorful character to draw based on the profiles developed. Take turns describing the characters. Describe personality traits as well as physical attributes. Discuss ways to visually convey these character traits.

5. On paper, draw detailed character sketches. Use facial expression, body language, and background to convey the personality.

**Process:**
**Session 3**
**30-45 min.**

### Paint character sketches

6. Paint sketches with watercolors. Use bold, contrasting colors for strong visibility or pastels to depict timidity, for example. Air-dry the paintings.

**Process:**
**Session 4**
**20-30 min.**

### Create text for poster

7. Together, consider how to "advertise" the characters on a "Wanted" poster. List information such as:
Name_____
AKA (Also known as) _____
Last seen at _____
Physical characteristics _____
Character traits_____
Other remarks _____
Encourage children to use words from their vocabulary lists.

8. Write a few words for each category. Check spellings. Copy descriptions on separate paper.

8. Identify information to feature on the "Wanted" poster. Draft a descriptive paragraph. Write the material neatly on separate paper.

**Process:**
**Session 5**
**20-30 min.**

### Design poster layout

9. On poster board, create a border for the poster. Add a big, bold title. Add embellishments, such as outlines on the character sketch or boxes around the text to emphasize details and add to the poster's unified look.

10. Try various arrangements of pictures and text. Keep in mind elements of design shown on posters on display. Select a balanced, visually appealing layout. Glue all parts to the poster.

**Assessment**

• Does the drawing use color, shape, line, and texture to convey both personality traits and physical characteristics?

• Does the project reflect basic principles of poster design with vivid, contrasting colors; strong images; and an attractive layout?

• Ask students to reflect on this lesson and write a DREAM statement to summarize the most important things they learned.

• Does the text include words that aptly describe character?

• Are more complex, precise vocabulary words used to aptly describe character?

**Extensions**

Compare and contrast the visual impact of different posters. What design techniques are especially effective in capturing and holding the viewer's attention?

Play charades using the character traits vocabulary. Identify what traits are being acted out—or even the character being portrayed if the literary figure is familiar to all students in the group.

Some students may prefer to prepare their poster text with a word processor, especially those with fine-motor skills challenges.

Establish a Rogues Gallery in the school library or other prominent location to encourage students to read the books.

Invite talented student writers to interview members of the community who have had interesting character-building experiences (a recent immigrant, a Peace Corps volunteer, a member of the ambulance squad, or someone who overcame a physical challenge, for example). Ask them to write biographies for the school newspaper using strong, precise vocabulary. Older students might even submit their stories to the local newspaper.

Crayola **Dream~Makers**
Building fun and creativity into standards-based learning

# Think Outside the Etymological Box

## Objectives

Students expand their vocabularies by learning the meanings and functions of words and how those are changed with prefixes and suffixes.

Students create colorful 3-D study aids to expand their use of vocabulary words.

Students correlate words to pictures and symbols.

## Multiple Intelligences

Bodily-kinesthetic
Linguistic
Spatial

## What Does It Mean?

**Etymology:** from the Greek *etymon* (true meaning) and *logos* (word or study), tracing the history of a word by breaking it down into parts

## National Standards

**Visual Arts Standard #2**
Using knowledge of structures and functions

**Visual Arts Standard #5**
Reflecting upon and assessing the characteristics and merits of their work and the work of others

**Visual Arts Standard #6**
Making connections between visual arts and other disciplines

**English Language Arts Standard #3**
Students apply a wide range of strategies to comprehend, interpret, evaluate, and appreciate texts. They draw on their prior experience, their interactions with other readers and writers, their knowledge of word meaning and of other texts, their word identification strategies, and their understanding of textual features (e.g., sound-letter correspondence, sentence structure, context, graphics).

**English Language Arts Standard #11**
Students participate as knowledgeable, reflective, creative, and critical members of a variety of literacy communities.

## Background Information

By learning the meaning and function of common prefixes and suffixes students can rapidly expand their word-attack skills. Many prefixes and suffixes have Greek or Latin origins. Some suffixes change a word's part of speech (adjective to adverb), tense (-ed, -ing), or degree (-er, -est).

The prefix *pre* means "before" or "ahead of." In this case, a prefix is a group of letters added before a root word that changes its meaning. Words using this prefix are *pretest*, *preview*, *prepare*. A study of prefixes often begins in first grade when the prefix *un* is introduced during a study of word opposites. *Re* (meaning *again*) is another common prefix for the early grades.

Students soon realize that learning basic prefixes gives them a clue to the meaning of unfamiliar words. Students who know that the prefix *hydro* means water can infer that *hydroelectricity* is electricity produced by water power. Knowing that *helio* refers to the sun enables students to determine a meaning for *heliotherapy*.

## Resources

*Prefixes and Suffixes: Systematic Sequential Phonics and Spelling* by Patricia Cunningham
Series of 120 systematic lessons for teaching phonics, spelling, and vocabulary through prefixes and suffixes.

*Quick and Easy Origami Boxes* by Tomoko Fuse
Attractive book includes a guide to basic origami symbols. Includes instructions for making boxes in squares, triangles, and hexagons. Clear step-by-step diagrams accompany close-up photographs showing the folding process as well as finished projects.

*Red Hot Root Words: Mastering Vocabulary With Prefixes, Suffixes, and Root Words* by Diane Draze
Manual for elementary teachers includes worksheets, games, and activities for students. Contains lists of vocabulary words and sample sentences demonstrating the use of targeted prefixes, suffixes, and roots. Similar book for grades 6 to 9 is also available.

*The American Heritage Children's Dictionary* from American Heritage Dictionaries
Child-friendly dictionary. More than 1,000 color photographs as well as information about the history of hundreds of words. Language Detective and Vocabulary Builder sections are very useful.

## Vocabulary List

*Use this list to explore new vocabulary, create idea webs, or brainstorm related subjects.*

- Prefixes

| | |
|---|---|
| Bene- (benefit) | Il-, in- (illegal, inappropriate) |
| Biblio- (bibliography) | Im- (import) |
| Bio- (biography) | Inter- (interrupt) |
| Circum- (circumference) | Per- (perforate) |
| Cogn- (cognition) | Post- (postscript) |
| Dict- (dictate) | Pre- (preview) |
| Ex- (exit) | Re- (rewrite) |
| Geo- (geography) | Semi- (semisweet) |
| Hemi- (hemisphere) | Sub- (submarine) |
| Hydro- (hydrophobia) | Syn-, sym- (symmetrical) |
| Hyper- (hyperactive) | Trans- (transport) |
| Hypo- (hypodermic) | |

- Suffixes

| | |
|---|---|
| - ful (cupful) | - phobia (claustrophobia) |
| - less (careless) | - phone (telephone) |
| - nym (synonym) | - port (transport) |
| - ology (biology) | - scope (microscope) |

- Art vocabulary

| | |
|---|---|
| Border | Sphere |
| Cube | Template |
| Pattern | Texture |

Artwork by students from
St. Jane Frances De Chantal School,
Easton, Pennsylvania.
Teacher: Julie Piazza

Artwork by students from
Klatt Elementary School,
Anchorage, Alaska.
Teacher: Barbara Yanoshek

Artwork by students from
Mt. Prospect Elementary School,
Basking Ridge, New Jersey.
Teacher: Regina DeFrancisco

Crayola Dream-Makers®
Building fun and creativity into standards-based learning

# Think Outside the Etymological Box

| | K-2 | 3-4 | 5-6 |
|---|---|---|---|
| **Suggested Preparation and Discussion** | Ascertain that children understand the concept of simple word opposites by reviewing pairs such as *tall/short* and *hot/cold*.<br><br>Challenge students to think of opposites for words such as *tie* or *lock*. Explain how adding the prefix *un-* changes the meaning of a word to its opposite. Ask them to think of other such words.<br><br>Together, list several familiar prefixes and their meanings. | Show students several familiar words with the same prefix. Ask them to identify and define the prefix (untie, unlock, unhappy). Who can explain what a prefix is? (something added to the beginning of a word that changes its meaning)<br><br>Together, list and define some common prefixes. Post the list. Explain how knowing the meanings of common prefixes can aid in defining new words.<br><br>Present an unfamiliar word or phrase such as *postoperative complications*. Challenge students to define it based on their knowledge of prefix meanings.<br><br>Ask what something similar to a prefix that is added to the end of a word is called. Explain that a suffix affects a word by changing its meaning, its part of speech, or its degree. | |

Examine sample art projects similar to those students will make. Discuss the unique structure of a cube. Ask students how they use and see cubes daily.

| | |
|---|---|
| **Crayola® Supplies** | • Colored Pencils   • Markers   • Model Magic®   • School Glue   • Scissors |
| **Other Materials** | • Oak tag |
| **Set-up/Tips** | • Invite parent volunteers or advanced students to prepare oak tag cube templates for the entire class. Cube templates can be found by conducting a search on the Web.<br><br>• This is an excellent small-group activity. Each small group makes one rolling cube and individual word cubes. |

**Japanese Decorative Paper Box**
Artist unknown
Painted decorative paper
3 1/2" x 5 x 4"
Private Collection.

**Kenyan Decorative Box**
Artist unknown
Ikat fabric and leather
2 1/2" x 3" x 10"
Private Collection.

**Blue Scarab With Hieroglyphics**
Artist unknown
Painted stone
3" x 1" x 3"
Private Collection.

| | K-2 | 3-4 | 5-6 |
|---|---|---|---|

**Process: Session 1 10 min.**

### Create rolling cubes

1. Roll a tennis ball-size Model Magic® sphere.
2. Press the sphere on a flat surface to form a six-sided cube. Air-dry the cube at least 24 hours.

**Process: Session 2 10 min.**

### Finish rolling cubes

3. Students choose six different prefixes (or suffixes for grades 3-6) from a recent vocabulary lesson. Write one on each side of the cube with markers.

**Process: Session 3 45-60 min.**

### Design word cubes

4. Students roll prefix or suffix cube to determine the affix to use for their word cubes. If necessary, roll again so each person in the group uses a different prefix or suffix.
5. Place cube templates flat on desks. In one square, write the prefix or suffix that was rolled. Use large letters.
6. Think of five different words that contain that prefix or suffix. Check a dictionary to make sure the chosen words actually contain prefixes or suffixes and are not just words that happen to contain the same letters as the given prefix or suffix (deflate vs. definition).
7. On each of the five remaining squares, write one word, illustrate it, and either define or write a sentence using the word. Add decorative borders using interesting textures and patterns.
8. Fold the template to create a cube with the artwork on the outside. Glue the cube together. Air-dry the glue before using the cube.

**Process: Session 4 10-15 min.**

### Share word cubes

9. Students examine classmates' cubes. What additional words using the key prefixes or suffixes can they generate? Encourage discussion. Display cubes in the classroom.

**Assessment**

- Do all words on the cube contain the given prefix or suffix?
- Are prefixes (or suffixes) and sample words clearly written and correctly spelled?
- Do sample sentences demonstrate an understanding of word usage?
- Do illustrations accurately reflect word meanings?
- Does decorative art add visual interest to the project?
- Ask students to reflect on this lesson and write a DREAM statement to summarize the most important things they learned.

**Extensions**

Limit the number of prefixes presented to younger students and those with learning needs.

Consider working with rhyming words and syllables.

Modify this activity as needed for kindergarten and some first grade students by putting letters or consonant blends on the rolling cube. Each student writes the letter or blend rolled and five words that start with that letter or blend on the word cube (ch: chin, church, chat, chain, cheerful).

Or choose common word endings that can be combined with a variety of beginning consonants (-at, -in, -am).

Instead of paper cubes, use small recycled boxes with lids glued closed. Cover with paper and fill with vocabulary as described.

Encourage students to look for words in newspapers or their independent reading books that contain prefixes they studied.

Children who are skilled at spatial relationships may want to create their own cubes.

Integrate vocabulary study with a math lesson on numerical prefixes such as: uno-, mono-, bi-, tri-, quad-, pent-, hex-, sept-, oct-, nove-, deci-, centi-, and milli-.

Challenge highly motivated students to research why September, October, November, and December seem to have been misnamed.

Offer students an opportunity to work with irregular plurals on their cubes: knife-knives; life-lives; wife-wives.

Have students consider working with pronoun referents such as: John saw a man. = He saw a man.

Make a Cube

- Use 90 lb., 8 ½" x 11" paper.
- Scale up diagram to paper size.
- Cut along the edges and decorate squares.
- Score and fold along all dotted lines.
- Apply glue to flaps.
- Fold squares and glued flaps to create a cube.

Crayola Dream~Makers®
Building fun and creativity into standards-based learning

# Kudos to Heroes and Heroines!

## Objectives

Students identify the characteristics of a hero or heroine by reflecting on personal experiences, reading, and/or research.

Students creatively sculpt medallions and write detailed certificates to award to a heroic individual they identified.

## Multiple Intelligences

| Interpersonal | Linguistic |
| --- | --- |

## National Standards

**Visual Arts Standard #3**
Choosing and evaluating a range of subject matter, symbols, and ideas

**Visual Arts Standard #4**
Understanding the visual arts in relation to history and cultures

**English Language Arts Standard #7**
Students conduct research on issues and interests by generating ideas and questions, and by posing problems. They gather, evaluate, and synthesize data from a variety of sources (e.g., print and non-print texts, artifacts, people) to communicate their discoveries in ways that suit their purpose and audience.

## What Does It Mean?

**Medallion:** an ornament resembling a medal, often used to recognize a person's greatness

**Score:** notch, scratch, or indent

## Background Information

Throughout the world, heroes and heroines are recognized. These individuals can be athletes who compete in the Olympic Games; scholars or scientists who are recognized with Nobel Prizes; or ordinary citizens who, when confronted by extraordinary circumstances, put the safety and welfare of others ahead of their own.

Medals and medallions are often presented to soldiers for their heroism. In 1864, during the Civil War, Union General Benjamin Butler awarded medals to approximately 300 African American troops under his command out of appreciation for their heroism and bravery in confronting their enemies in battles for freedom.

Each year on the fourth of July a distinguished individual in the United States is presented the Freedom Award, which is a medallion. Like the United States, many other countries have a long history of their leaders presenting medallions to individuals for their great achievements.

## Resources

*Character Education: Grades K-6 Year 1* by John Heidel, Marion Lyman Mersereau, and Jennifer E. Jenke
Addresses nine universal values such as responsibility and respect with stories of heroes and heroines from various cultures. Includes suggestions for lessons and community service projects.

*Kids With Courage: True Stories About Young People Making a Difference* by Barbara A. Lewis
Stories of 18 young people to inspire older elementary students.

*Teammates* by Peter Golenbock and Paul Bacon
All elementary students will be captivated to learn about Jackie Robinson and PeeWee Reese, the teammate who honored him before a hostile crowd. Leads to discussions of friendship, courage, and racial harmony.

*Using Picture Story Books to Teach Character Education* by Susan Hall
Background information for teachers on character education. Includes annotated bibliographies of picture books that address more than 20 positive character traits.

## Vocabulary List

*Use this list to explore new vocabulary, create idea webs, or brainstorm related subjects.*

- Art vocabulary

| | | |
| --- | --- | --- |
| Accolade | Form | Sculpt |
| Award | Medallion | Shape |
| Design | Pattern | Texture |
| Emphasis | Relief | |

- Heroic character traits

| | | |
| --- | --- | --- |
| Brave | Constant | Innovative |
| Compassionate | Courageous | Perseverant |
| Competent | Daring | Selfless |
| | Diligent | Stalwart |
| | Empathetic | Trustworthy |
| | Exceptional | Unafraid |
| | Exemplary | Unselfish |
| | Forgiving | Valiant |
| | Generous | |

**Man in the Maze Pendant**
Circa 1900s
Artist: Marvin Lucas, Hopi
Silver
Private Collection.

The Man in the Maze pendant shows a figure with hands raised. This figure symbolizes that man successfully navigated through life. Find similar examples to show students how symbols are used to reflect meaning in both medals and designs found in certificates.

great work

1#

Thanks for making peace.

1#

To Martin Lythet King, J For making peace to the Blacks an Whites!!!

great work

Thank YOU For Being a Brave, and Diligent Soldier

This Award Is Presented To
For Taking Care Of The World's Fish Population
January 21, 2525

BEST FISHER

World Heroine 2020

Friendly, Caring And Nice!!

Artwork by students from Asa Packer Elementary School, Bethlehem, Pennsylvania.
Teacher: Linda Kondikoff

"People of the Year" magazine cover design artwork by students from St. Theresa School, Hellertown, Pennsylvania.

Crayola Dream~Makers®
Building fun and creativity into standards-based learning

# Kudos to Heroes and Heroines!

| | K-2 | 3-4 | 5-6 |
|---|---|---|---|
| **Suggested Preparation and Discussion** | Display pictures of medals and awards and "people of the year" magazine covers of heroic individuals as well as several children's books that focus on heroism. Lead a discussion to compare and contrast the people in the display. Consider questions such as, What design elements are commonly used? How does each award reflect the specific character trait(s) of the person being recognized? What symbols and descriptive adjectives are used?<br><br>Discuss *Teammates* or similar literature about heroic action with the students. Share personal or local heroic adventures.<br><br>With students, create a bulletin board banner titled "Criteria for Heroism." Write questions on index cards and post under the headline. Who are some heroes or heroines in students' own lives? Who are some famous ones? What character traits do these people possess? | | |
| **Crayola® Supplies** | • Model Magic®  • Markers | • Air-Dry Clay or Model Magic<br>• Paint Brushes  • Tempera Paint | • Markers |
| | • Colored Pencils | | |
| **Other Materials** | • Modeling tools such as craft sticks or plastic dinnerware<br>• Plastic drinking straws  • Recycled newspaper  • Ribbon<br>• Textured surfaces such as sink mats  • Water containers | | • Stapler & staples |
| | • Drawing paper | | |
| **Set-up/Tips** | • Model Magic compound fresh from the pack sticks to itself.<br>• Sculpt air-dry clay on paper plates. As needed, dampen and score surfaces to be attached. Rub medallions with a moist, paint-filled sponge to soften the etched designs and words.<br>• Cover painting surface with newspaper. | | |
| **Process: Session 1 15-20 min.** | **Identify heroic words**<br>1. Students share heroic adventures they know about and understand.<br>2. List words that describe heroes and heroines.<br>3. Choose one person to honor as a hero or heroine. Pick descriptive words and symbols for creating medallions and certificates. | | **Compare and contrast heroic words**<br>1. Research and share descriptions of heroic acts. Track the different types of acts found and other common information.<br>2. Compare and contrast words that are used to describe these heroic acts. List words that are used repeatedly. |
| **Process: Session 2 40-50 min. or more** | **Create medallions**<br>4. Press a tennis-ball amount of modeling compound into a flat disc. Press the disc against textured surfaces to create patterns on both sides. Trim the sides with a modeling tool. Smooth with fingers.<br>5. Use a pencil point to etch heroic words and symbols—or sculpt and add separate 3-D symbols—to the medallion surface. More mature students' medallions are increasingly elaborate and detailed.<br>6. Push a straw through the top of the medallion. Twist to make a hole for a ribbon. Air-dry Model Magic compound at least 24 hours. Air-dry the clay for 3 days. | | **Create magazine covers**<br>3. Look at "people of the year" magazine covers on display. Point out text, illustrations, photographs, and other relevant details.<br>4. Sketch cover designs for a magazine cover that features headlines using the identified words and illustrations.<br>5. In teams, discuss the cover designs. Select one design to embellish. Each team member redesigns a magazine cover using markers. Display designs from each team. |

| | K-2 | 3-4 | 5-6 |
|---|---|---|---|
| **Process: Session 3 15-20 min.** | **Decorate medals** <br> 7. Decorate medals with markers (grades K-2) or paint (grades 3-4). Air-dry the paint. <br> 8. Bend a ribbon in half and pull the loop through the ribbon hole. Thread both ends of the ribbon through the loop. Pull the ribbon closed. | | **Write oral presentations** <br> 6. Write feature articles that include heroic words identified in the research. Exchange with other students on the team to proofread. Revise accordingly. <br> 7. Read articles to the class and show cover designs. Students comment on the clarity and detail of articles as well as effectiveness of cover illustrations. <br> 8. Based on class feedback, teams each select a cover and article to publish. |
| **Process: Session 4 45-50 min.** | **Design a certificate** <br> 9. Write and illustrate a paper award certificate. Use heroic vocabulary as well as signs and symbols that reflect the nature of the award. Include lines, shapes, colors, textures, and patterns in decorative borders. | | **Publish cover and writings** <br> 9. Make black and white photocopies of the cover design and article. Hand color them with colored pencil. <br> 10. Staple the cover to article for distribution. |
| **Assessment** | • Does the medallion design make use of visual symbols that accurately depict a heroic achievement? Do the heroic individual's accomplishments reflect the character traits of a hero or heroine? <br> • Does the vocabulary on the certificate include some words that are common when talking about heroic individuals? In the case of older students, has an attempt been made to use more advanced vocabulary? Are all words spelled correctly? | | • Did students work cooperatively in small groups to design covers? Were students receptive to feedback from others? <br> • Were article drafts proofread and edited? Are they clearly written and descriptive about the individual? <br> • How effective were cover designs in portraying the individuals? |
| | • Did students follow directions to create their medallions, certificates, magazine covers, and feature articles? <br> • Ask students to reflect on this lesson and write a DREAM statement to summarize the most important things they learned. | | |
| **Extensions** | Students plan and hold an awards ceremony. Invite honorees if they are friends, relatives, or live in the community. If students made awards for heroes they read about in books, showcase the books and awards together in the school library. <br><br> More advanced students might each research a person whom they admire and then role play an awards ceremony where their heroes make acceptance speeches for their awards. <br><br> As an aid to young students and students with special needs, display key words in a prominent place in the classroom. <br><br> Offer students with small-motor coordination challenges the opportunity to create text for their awards on a computer. Add colorful details to the printed certificate with markers or colored pencils. | | |

Artwork by students from
Asa Packer Elementary School,
Bethlehem, Pennsylvania.
Teacher: Linda Kondikoff

Crayola **Dream~Makers**
Building fun and creativity into standards-based learning

# Choosing Crayola Art Supplies

The lessons in this guide suggest types of art materials. This chart outlines the specific characteristics of different Crayola art materials. Use it to choose which variation best meets your needs and those of your students. Crayola products are subject to change. Check Crayola.com for the most recent information.

| CRAYONS/OIL PASTELS | CHARACTERISTICS |
|---|---|
| Regular Crayons (3-5/8" x 5/16") | • Brilliant colors; smooth, even color lay down. |
| Large Size Crayons (4" x 7/16") | • Brilliant colors; smooth, even color lay down.<br>• Larger size for younger child palm grip. |
| Triangular Crayons | • Brilliant colors; smooth, even color lay down.<br>• Triangular shape helps guide correct pincer grip.<br>• Anti-roll. |
| Washable Crayons | • Brilliant colors; smooth, even color lay down.<br>• Available in regular, large, and triangular sizes.<br>• Superior washability from walls, tables, and most surfaces. |
| Construction Paper™ Crayons | • Brilliant colors; smooth, even color lay down.<br>• Color shows on dark paper, brown craft paper, and similar surfaces. |
| Fabric Crayons | • Permanent when drawing is heat transferred to synthetic fabric. |
| Twistables® Crayons | • Brilliant colors; smooth, even color lay down.<br>• Durable plastic barrel.<br>• No sharpening with easy twist-up action. |
| Twistables Erasable Crayons | • Complete erasability of marks.<br>• Brilliant colors; smooth, even color lay down.<br>• Durable plastic barrel.<br>• No sharpening with easy twist-up action.<br>• Eraser on each crayon. |
| Twistables Slick Stix™ Crayons | • Super-smooth color glides on paper.<br>• Water soluble upon application.<br>• Dries quickly with no smearing.<br>• Durable plastic barrel.<br>• Great for older student crayon techniques.<br>• Appropriate for students with special needs due to ease of color lay down. |
| Oil Pastels | • Opaque colors blend easily.<br>• Good color lay down.<br>• Hexagonal shape prevents rolling. |
| Portfolio® Series Oil Pastels | • Opaque colors blend and layer well, with velvety lay down.<br>• Unique water solubility allows watercolor washes. |

| MARKERS | CHARACTERISTICS |
|---|---|
| Regular Markers | • Bright, brilliant, transparent colors.<br>• Conical tip draws thick and thin lines.<br>• Fine tip draws thin lines and detail. |
| Washable Markers | • Washability you can trust™–superior washability from hands and most clothing.<br>• Bright, brilliant, transparent colors.<br>• Conical tip draws thick and thin lines.<br>• Fine tip draws thin lines and detail.<br>• Wedge tip provides ease in broad strokes and vertical applications. |
| Gel Markers | • Bright, opaque colors that deliver bold marks on black and dark papers.<br>• World's most washable marker with superior washability from hands and most clothing.<br>• Writes on glass, foil, glossy, and other non-porous surfaces.<br>• Conical tip draws thick and thin lines. |
| Overwriters® Markers | • Bright "overcolors" magically color over darker "undercolors" for exciting and dramatic effects. |
| Color Changeables™ Markers | • Students have fun seeing colors magically "pop out" over each other for new creative expression possibilities.<br>• Increased color variety as "wand" changes 7 colors to 7 new colors. |
| Twistables Markers | • No lost caps!<br>• Bright, brilliant, transparent colors. |
| Fabric Markers | • Permanent bright color on cotton or cotton blends when heat set.<br>• Bullet tip for medium and fine detail. |
| Dry-Erase Markers | • Low odor, bold color that can be viewed from a distance.<br>• Chisel and bullet tips. |

| COLORED PENCILS | CHARACTERISTICS |
|---|---|
| Colored Pencils | • Bright, vivid colors with opaque lay down.<br>• Good blending.<br>• Thick 3 mm colored core; made from reforested wood. |
| Watercolor Colored Pencils | • Water soluble for watercolor and drawing effects.<br>• Bright, vivid colors with opaque lay down.<br>• Good blending.<br>• Thick 3 mm colored core; made from reforested wood. |
| Erasable Colored Pencils | • Complete erasability of pencil marks.<br>• Bright colors with opaque lay down.<br>• Good blending.<br>• Eraser on each pencil.<br>• Thick 3 mm colored core; made from reforested wood. |
| Twistables Colored Pencils | • Bright colors; smooth, even color lay down.<br>• Durable plastic barrel.<br>• No sharpening with easy twist-up action. |
| Twistables Erasable Colored Pencils | • Complete erasability of pencil marks.<br>• Bright colors; smooth, even color lay down.<br>• Durable plastic barrel.<br>• No sharpening with easy twist-up action.<br>• Eraser on each pencil. |
| Write Start® Colored Pencils | • Thick 5.3 mm colored core and large hexagonal barrels are great for young students.<br>• Bright, vivid colors with opaque lay down.<br>• Anti-roll.<br>• Made from reforested wood. |

| MODELING COMPOUNDS | CHARACTERISTICS |
|---|---|
| Air-Dry Clay | • No firing, air-dry clay.<br>• Good for high-detail projects.<br>• Natural clay body to create solid, durable forms.<br>• Suitable for all clay techniques.<br>• White color suitable for all color/surface decoration.<br>• Air-dries hard. |
| Model Magic® | • Soft, easy-to-manipulate compound.<br>• Good for low-detail projects.<br>• Good for young students and those who are developing manual dexterity.<br>• Air-dries to consistency of a foam cup. |
| Modeling Clay | • Traditional oil-based clay.<br>• Non-hardening and reusable. |

| PAINTS | CHARACTERISTICS |
|---|---|
| Premier™ Tempera | • Ultimate opacity and coverage.<br>• Creamy consistency flows smoothly and will not crack or flake.<br>• Intense, true hues for accurate color mixing. |
| Artista II® value-priced Tempera | • Fine-quality colors with good opacity.<br>• Creamy consistency flows smoothly and will not crack or flake.<br>• Good hues for excellent color mixtures.<br>• Washable from skin and fabrics. |
| Washable Paint | • Washability you can trust™–superior washability from skin and fabrics.<br>• Bright, clean colors for consistent color mixing.<br>• Smooth-flowing formula will not crack or flake. |
| Acrylic Paint | • Pigment-rich colors are intense even when diluted; achieve accurate color mixes.<br>• Thick, tube-like viscosity, for a variety of techniques from air-brushing to impasto.<br>• Permanent, water resistant, and flexible when dry. |
| Washable Finger Paint | • Bright colors, thick consistency.<br>• Washable from skin and fabrics. |
| Watercolors | • Bright, intense, transparent colors.<br>• True hues for accurate color mixing.<br>• Ideal for opaque and transparent techniques. |
| Washable Watercolors | • Washability you can trust–superior washability from skin and fabrics.<br>• Bright, intense, transparent colors. |